Anticorruption in Transition
A Contribution to the Policy Debate

The World Bank
Washington, D.C.

Library of Congress Cataloging-in-Publication Data

Anticorruption in transition : confronting the challenge of state capture.
        p. cm.
    Includes bibliographical references.
    ISBN 0-8213-4802-7
        1. Political corruption—Europe, Eastern. 2. Political corruption—Former Soviet
        republics. 3. Privatization—Corrupt practices—Europe, Eastern. 4. Privatization—Corrupt
        practices—Former Soviet republics. I. World Bank.

    JN96.A56 C62 2000
    353.4′6—dc21   000-43982

TABLE OF CONTENTS

List of Text Boxes

List of Tables

List of Figures

Foreword

With the increasing recognition across the globe of the damaging effects of corruption on economic growth and social stability, the demand for practical strategies to reduce corruption has grown dramatically. The problem is not confined to any particular region, and developed, developing and transition countries alike are confronting these challenges. In the countries of Central and Eastern Europe, the Baltics, and the Commonwealth of Independent States, the simultaneous processes of developing a market economy, designing new political and social institutions and redistributing social assets have created fertile ground for corruption. Many governments throughout the region have made combating corruption a priority and have turned to the World Bank for assistance in designing feasible anticorruption strategies.

Our initial experience in providing anticorruption assistance has shown that while much is known about the proximate causes and consequences of corruption, we know comparatively little about the economic, political and historical factors underlying the *persistence* of corruption in the region. Moreover, we have seen through our assistance efforts that the extent and nature of the problem differ substantially across the transition countries requiring a differentiated approach to the prioritization and sequencing of reforms.

This report seeks to unbundle the varied practices of corruption to identify and compare different patterns of the problem across transition countries. It then draws out lessons for tailoring anticorruption strategies to address the variation across the region in an effort to target reforms more effectively. The report draws on a multitude of sources of ongoing research and lessons of experience, including the World Bank's work in this area. However, the report does not seek to review the World Bank's operations or set specific strategic guidelines for its operational work in this area. Instead, the report is intended as a contribution to the growing policy dialogue on developing practical strategies for reducing corruption. As more and more countries seek to implement anticorruption programs, it is critical for the World Bank and other institutions to continue to enhance this dialogue with both the lessons of experience and with new approaches designed to tackle the roots of corruption.

Johannes F. Linn
Vice President
Europe and Central Asia

Acknowledgments

The report was prepared by a core team led by Sanjay Pradhan and comprising James Anderson, Joel Hellman, Geraint Jones (EBRD and the World Bank), Bill Moore, Helga Muller, Randi Ryterman, and Helen Sutch.

The report benefited from a large number of contributions both from within the World Bank and from external partners. The analysis and measurement of state capture, first published in the *EBRD Transition Report 1999*, is based on a collaborative research project between the Policy Studies Programme of the EBRD and the World Bank (WBI) under the direction of Joel Hellman and Daniel Kaufmann, who also provided important advice and inputs. We are grateful to the Office of the Chief Economist of the EBRD for their partnership.

Contributors from the World Bank include: Luba Beardsley, Sandra Bloemenkamp, Harry Broadman, Lilia Burunciuc, Peter Dean, Jean-Jacques Dethier, Nora Dudwick, Itzhak Goldberg, Christine Jones, Alma Kanani, Vitaliy Kartamychev, Ioannis Kessides, Kathleen Kuehnast, Kathy Lalazarian, Maureen Lewis, Laszlo Lovei, Alexandre Marc, Allister Moon, Amitabha Mukherjee, Mark Nelson, Madeleine O'Donnell, Jana Orac, Neil Parison, Friedrich Peloschek, Alexey Proskuryakov, Francesca Recanatini, Gary Reid, Ana Revenga, Sue Rutledge, Mary Sheehan, Maria Shkaratan, Rick Stapenhurst, Margret Thalwitz, Peter Thomson, Cari Votava, Shang-Jin Wei, and Deborah Wetzel. Lilian Canamaso, Valery Ciancio, Miranda Cookson, and Virginia Sapinoso provided administrative support.

External contributors include: Vladimir Brovkin (US; Transnational Center for Crime and Corruption), Milan Cech (The Czech Republic; Police), Bertrand de Speville (consultant, former Commissioner of Hong Kong Independent Commission Against Corruption), Pavol Fric (The Czech Republic; Charles University), Irina Borisovna Garsia (The Russian Federation; RIA Novosty Agency), Fiona Harrison (UK; Article 19), Keith Henderson (US; Transnational Center for Crime and Corruption), Leslie Holmes (Australia; University of Melbourne), Serhyi Holovati (Ukraine; President of the Ukrainian Legal Foundation; Member of Parliament; former Minister of Justice), Evzen Kocenda (The Czech Republic; CERGE), Lubomir Lizal (The Czech Republic; CERGE), Mario Nuti (UK; London Business School), Sam Paul (Consultant), Mark Philp (UK; University of Oxford), Martin Rhodes (European University Institute), Emilia Sicakova (The Slovak Republic; Transparency International), Vladimir Svetozarov (The Russian Federation; National Press Institute), Emil Tsenkov (Bulgaria; Coalition 2000), Joel Turkewitz (Consultant), Janine Wedel (Consultant), Daniela Zemanovicova (The Slovak Republic; Transparency International).

An interim, summary version of this document was reviewed by ECA's External Advisory Board (EAB) on Governance. The EAB is chaired by Professor Leszek Balcerowowicz (Poland; then Deputy Prime Minister and Minister of Finance), and consists of 16 distinguished individuals from government, academia, NGOs and the private sector: Vladimir Gligorov (Macedonia; Research Fellow; Wiener Institut fuer Internationale Wirtschaftsvergleiche); Serhiy Holovaty (Ukraine; President of the Ukrainian Legal Foundation; Member of Parliament; former Minister of Justice); Lena Kolarska-Bobinska (Poland; Director of Institute of Public Affairs); Miklos Marshall (Hungary; Transparency International); Ivan Miklos (Slovak Republic; Deputy Prime

Minister); Vira Nanivska (Ukraine; Director, International Center for Policy Studies (ICPS)); Professor Richard Pipes (U.S.; Harvard University); Alexandre Rondeli (Georgia; Director, International Policy Research and Analysis Center, Ministry of Foreign Affairs); Georgyi Satarov (The Russian Federation; President of the Indem Foundation (Infomatics for Democracy), former Assistant to President Boris Yeltsin); Daulet Sembayev (Kazakhstan; Chairman of the Association of Financiers of Kazakhstan, Chairman, Advisory Board, Kazkommertsbank); Valeriu Stoica (Romania; Deputy Prime Minister, Minister of Justice); Vita Terauda (Latvia; Executive Director of Soros Foundation, former Minister of State Reform); Ugnius Trumpa (Lithuania; Vice President, Lithuanian Free Market Institute); Laszlo Urban (Hungary; Deputy CEO of Postabank); and Dimitrii Vasiliev (Russia; Chairman, Institute for Corporate Governance).

The document has been reviewed by the ECA Regional Management Team chaired by Johannes Linn, by the Public Sector Board chaired by Cheryl Gray (internal peer reviewer), and by Professor Susan Rose-Ackerman (external peer reviewer, Yale University). Written comments were provided by: Basil Kavalsky, Brian Levy, Nick Manning, Rick Messick, Pradeep Mitra, Ian Newport, Marcelo Selowsky, Shekhar Shah, and Andrew Vorkink.

The participation of more than 3,000 enterprise managers in the Business Environment and Enterprise Performance Survey (BEEPS), and the participation of NGOs in 17 transition countries in a brief survey on civil society, are gratefully acknowledged. The BEEPS was conducted and financed by the Policy Studies Programme of the EBRD and the Word Bank Institute. The support of Nicholas Stern and Steven Fries of the EBRD is gratefully acknowledged.

The authors would like to thank the Danish, Italian, and Norwegian Governments, UK-DFID, and USAID for their financial support.

Abbreviations

ACER	Albanian Center for Economic Research
AIDS	Acquired Immune Deficiency Syndrome
BEEPS	Business Environment and Enterprise Performance Survey
CEE	Central and Eastern Europe
CIS	Commonwealth of Independent States
EBRD	European Bank for Reconstruction and Development
EU	European Union
FDI	Foreign Direct Investment
FSU	Former Soviet Union
GDP	Gross Domestic Product
GORBI	Georgian Opinion Research Business International
KGB	Komitet Gosudarstvennoy Bezopasnosti
NGOs	Non-Governmental Organizations
OECD	Organisation for Economic Co-operation and Development
SMEs	Small- and Medium-sized Enterprises
SOEs	State Owned Enterprises
UK	United Kingdom
UNICRI	United Nations Interregional Crime and Justice Research Institute
US	United States
USAID	United States Agency for International Development
USD	United States Dollar
WBI	World Bank Institute

Executive Summary

More than a decade into the simultaneous political and economic transitions in Eastern Europe and the former Soviet Union, dynamic market economies have been created and states have been reshaped, but the boundaries between state and economy remain murky. The fusion of the state and the economy that characterized the communist system has been replaced in most of the countries by a new order, but one in which the separation of private and public interests has not been adequately defined. Corruption in the region is developing new dimensions, reaching new heights, and posing new challenges.

The transition countries have been engaged in a concentrated process of defining the basic rules and institutions to govern their economies and societies, while at the same time redistributing the bulk of their assets. In many countries, corruption has had a significant impact on this process, encoding advantages in these new rules and institutions for narrow vested interests and distorting the path of economic and political development. Media reports throughout the region tell of powerful firms and individual "oligarchs" buying off politicians and bureaucrats to shape the legal, policy, and regulatory environments in their own interests. Numerous high-profile corruption scandals have revealed politicians abusing their authority to shift public resources to themselves and their allies through well-hidden stakes in a complex web of private and public companies. In many countries, the public perceives corruption to be woven into the basic institutional framework, undermining governance and weakening the credibility of the state.

These public perceptions of pervasive corruption in parts of the region are supported by a wide range of international comparisons. A summary of 12 of the most widely known international corruption indices, depicted in Figure 1, suggests that perceptions of corruption in the Commonwealth of Independent States (CIS) are among the highest of all countries included. While corruption levels in the countries of Central and Eastern Europe and the Baltics (CEE) are lower, they are still on par with the countries of Latin America and the Middle East, at levels considerably higher than those in the OECD countries.

Figure 1. World-wide Perceptions of Corruption

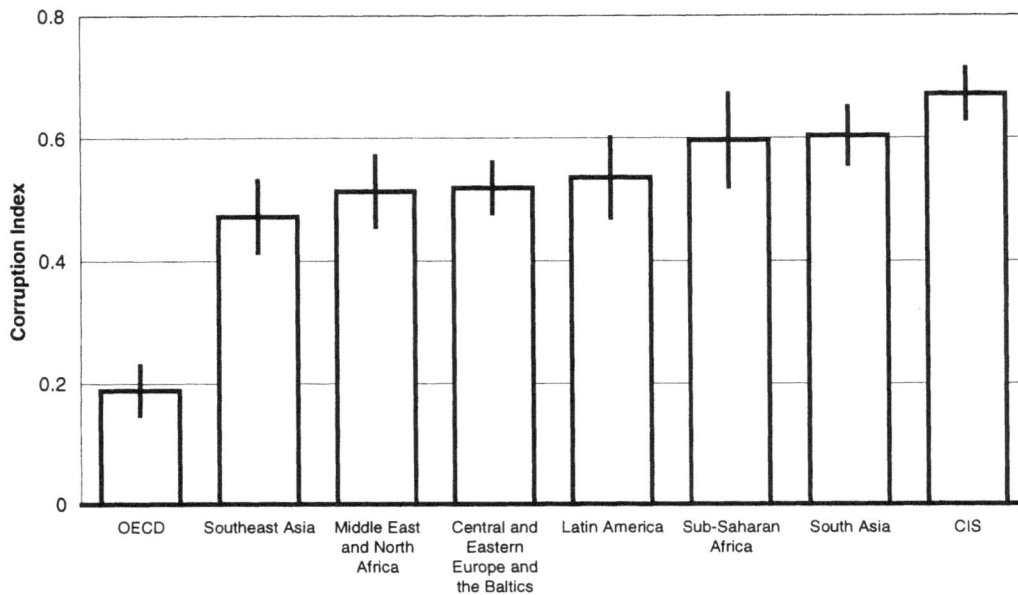

The thin line at the top of each bar represents the statistical margin of error (based on a single standard deviation) calculated on the basis of the aggregated indicators. Source: Kaufmann, Kraay, and Zoido-Labaton (1999a). See Annex 1 for a description of the calculation of this summary index and the margins of error.

The expansion of corruption in the decade of transition has coincided with a sharp, initial decline in output and significantly higher levels of poverty and inequality across the region. Though unraveling the lines of causality may be difficult, recent empirical studies have documented the considerable economic and social costs of corruption. One conclusion of these studies raises particular concern: it is the poor who bear the heaviest brunt of corruption. Corruption weakens public service delivery, misdirects public resources, and holds back the growth that is necessary to pull people out of poverty. Stories abound of pension payments postponed and disability benefits denied, all because the requisite bribes were not paid. Measures of the aggregate social costs of the problem do not reveal the human suffering wrought by corruption.

In those countries where the problem is most entrenched, corruption undermines the driving forces behind reform. New firms are driven into the underground economy. Vital resources are siphoned off shore. Foreign investors turn away in frustration. As a result, some countries risk becoming trapped in a vicious circle in which pervasive corruption reduces public revenues, undermines public trust, and weakens the credibility of the state, unless decisive leadership can push through the necessary reforms.

Recognizing that corruption is one of the most serious obstacles to development, the World Bank has made combating corruption a central institutional priority. At the same time, a number of transition countries have begun to request assistance from the World Bank specifically to target corruption. Since 1997, the World Bank has intensively developed diagnostic tools, technical assistance, training programs, and lending instruments targeted toward reducing corruption in transition countries. This report does not focus on World Bank experience *per se*. Rather, it focuses on the diagnosis of corruption across transition countries and the implications for country strategies on the ground. The World Bank stands ready to support countries' anticorruption programs, in partnership with other domestic and international actors.

Though still in the early stages of development, the experience of anticorruption programs to date has produced mixed results. Ambitious anticorruption campaigns in several countries have floundered at the implementation stage. Key structural reforms have been blocked by powerful vested interests. In some cases, politicians have hijacked the anticorruption agenda and used it to attack their rivals. Governments in the region have tended to prefer strengthening enforcement mechanisms to addressing the structural roots of the problem. One reason for the difficulties has been an overemphasis on technocratic measures in a uniform approach that does not take into account important differences among countries in the power and concentration of vested interests, the capacity of the state, and the channels of accountability between the state and civil society.

Confronting corruption in transition countries requires a more complex approach that recognizes the diverse factors underlying the persistence of corruption and provides a foundation for tailoring strategies to the particular contours of the problem in different countries. This report provides an approach to meeting these challenges. It begins by unbundling the problem of corruption, recognizing that what is generally treated as a unidimensional phenomenon encompasses a range of different interactions within the state and between the state and society, each with its own dynamics. On this basis, a new typology of corruption is developed for the transition countries to explore differences in the origins and consequences of corruption in distinct groups of countries. Specific policy recommendations are then tailored for each group, drawing from a common set of institutional and policy reforms, with emphasis on how to target anticorruption efforts, how to sequence reforms, and how to calibrate realistic expectations in different contexts.

The report relies on an important new source of data on governance and corruption in transition economies—the 1999 Business Environment and Enterprise Performance Survey (BEEPS) commissioned jointly by the World Bank and the European Bank for Reconstruction and Development. The BEEPS is a firm-level survey of more than 3,000 enterprise owners and senior managers in 22 transition countries. It provides new and more robust measures of a number of forms of corruption across transition countries from the point of view of firms. In addition, data from a wealth of audit reports, empirical studies, cross-country household surveys, and detailed diagnostic studies in selected transition countries are also consulted to provide a broader picture of corruption from the perspectives of households and state officials. The combination of these studies with the BEEPS data provides a powerful and balanced foundation from which to understand the depth and contours of the problem of corruption within and across countries.

The Level and Pattern of Corruption in the Transition Countries

The report seeks to unbundle the phenomenon of corruption, placing primary emphasis on the distinction between state capture and administrative corruption. **State capture** refers to the actions of individuals, groups, or firms both in the public and private sectors *to influence the formation* of laws, regulations, decrees, and other government policies to their own advantage as a result of the illicit and non-transparent provision of private benefits to public officials. There are many different forms of the problem. Distinctions can be drawn between the types of institutions subject to capture—the legislature, the executive, the judiciary, or regulatory agencies and the types of actors engaged in the capturing—private firms, political leaders, or narrow interest groups. Yet all forms of state capture are directed toward extracting rents from the state for a narrow range of individuals, firms, or sectors through distorting the basic legal and regulatory framework with potentially enormous losses for the society at large. They thrive where economic power is highly concentrated, countervailing social interests are weak, and the formal channels of political influence and interest intermediation are underdeveloped.

By investigating the channels through which firms seek to influence the state, the BEEPS survey represents the first attempt to measure some aspects of the incidence of capture across the transition countries, albeit representing only the problem of capture by firms (as opposed to other individuals or groups). The survey identified a number of specific activities that fall within the definition of state capture, including: the "sale" of Parliamentary votes and presidential decrees to private interests; the sale of civil and criminal court decisions to private interests; corrupt mishandling of central bank funds; and illegal contributions by private actors to political parties. Firms were asked to assess the *direct impact* on their business from each of these activities, regardless of whether they engaged in such activities themselves. Thus, capture is measured not by how many firms engage in it, but by the share of firms whose business is directly affected by it. Figure 2 presents an aggregate index of the impact of state capture across the transition countries based on the dimensions listed above.

Figure 2. State Capture Index *(share of firms affected by state capture)*

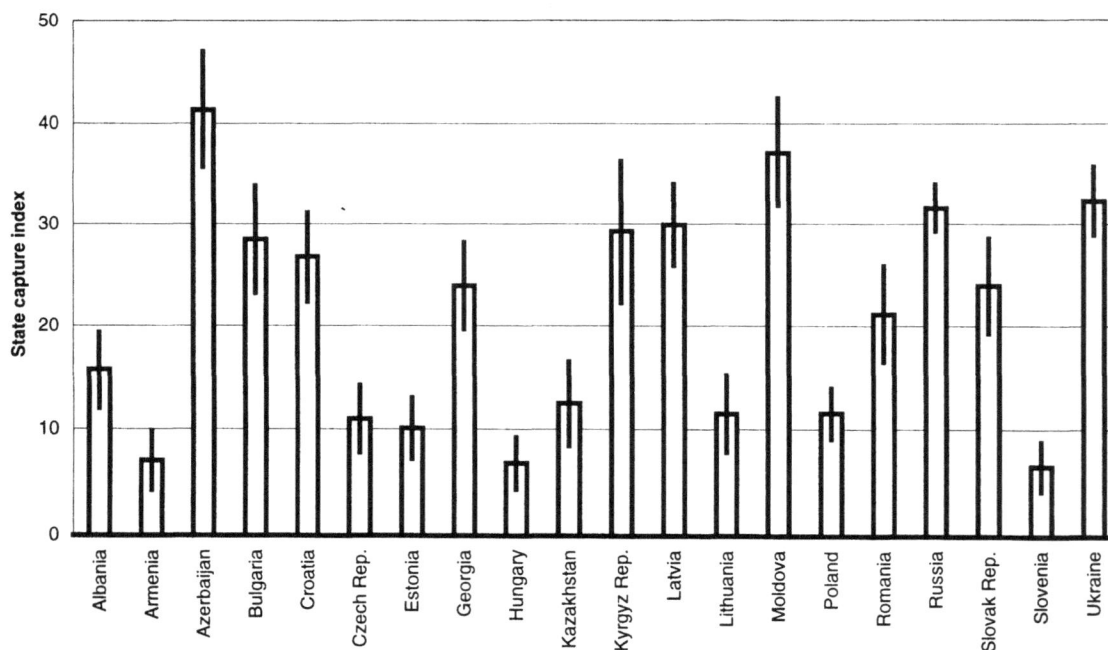

The thin line at the top of each bar represents the statistical margin of error (based on a single standard deviation) calculated for each country within the sample. Source: Hellman, Jones, and Kaufmann (2000a).

While state capture encodes advantages for particular individuals or groups in the basic legal or regulatory framework, **administrative corruption** refers to the intentional imposition of distortions in the prescribed *implementation* of existing laws, rules, and regulations to provide advantages to either state or non-state actors as a result of the illicit and non-transparent provision of private gains to public officials. The classic example of administrative corruption is that of a hapless shop owner forced to pay bribes to a seemingly endless stream of official inspectors to overlook minor (or possibly major) infractions of existing regulations. Beyond such forms of extortion, administrative corruption also includes such familiar examples of "grease payments" as bribes to gain licenses, to smooth customs procedures, to win public procurement contracts, or to be given priority in the provision of a variety of other government services. Finally, state officials can simply misdirect public funds under their control for their own or their family's direct financial benefit. At the root of this form of corruption is discretion on the part of public officials to grant selective exemptions, to prioritize the delivery of public services, or to discriminate in the application of rules and regulations.

The BEEPS survey also provides data to develop an aggregate measure of administrative corruption across the transition countries. Firms estimated the share of their revenues that they typically pay per annum in unofficial payments to public officials in order to "get things done." The average bribe share by country is presented in Figure 3.

Figure 3. Administrative Corruption
(bribes as a share of annual revenues)

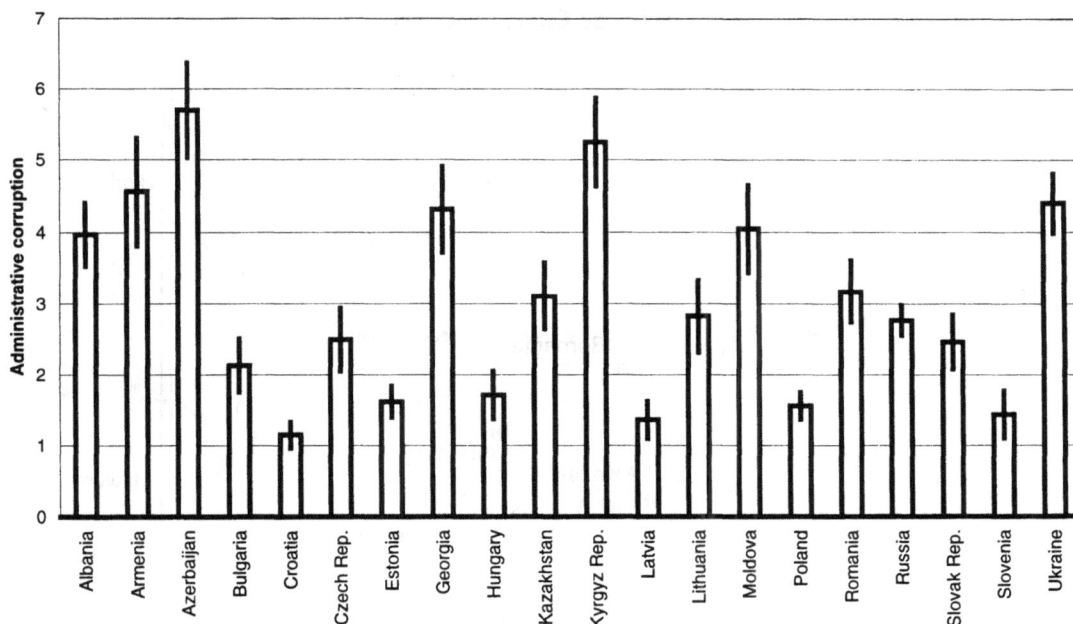

The thin line at the top of each bar represents the statistical margin of error (based on a single standard deviation) calculated for each country within the sample. Source: BEEPS.

xviii

Across the CIS, average payments for administrative corruption constitute 3.7 percent of firm revenues; the share falls to 2.2 percent of revenues in CEE. Yet measuring administrative corruption as a share of firm revenues does not convey the full weight of the burden of this form of corruption. Based on a rough estimate of profit margins across the region, firms in countries with the highest levels of administrative corruption can pay up to 25 percent of their profits in such payments.

As the BEEPS survey measures only some of the diverse forms of state capture and administrative corruption, it undoubtedly underestimates the extent of both problems across the region. Neither form of corruption is limited exclusively to acts initiated by or involving private sector firms. Public officials themselves can misuse their authority to shape the rules of the game or to distort the implementation of state policy to benefit their own private financial interests. This problem of conflict of interest spans both types of corruption, especially in transition countries. Though all countries in the region (as well as most advanced countries across the globe) continue to have problems with both state capture and administrative corruption, the report demonstrates that the nature and variation of their interaction in the context of transition raises different challenges for developing effective anticorruption strategies.

The report presents a typology of corruption based on the interaction of state capture and administrative corruption. Figure 4 shows a two-by-two matrix of countries with each axis ranging from "high" to "medium" denoting the relative level of each form of corruption. The term "medium" is chosen as a reminder that both administrative corruption and state capture continue to be serious problems in every country of the region.

Figure 4. Typology of Corruption

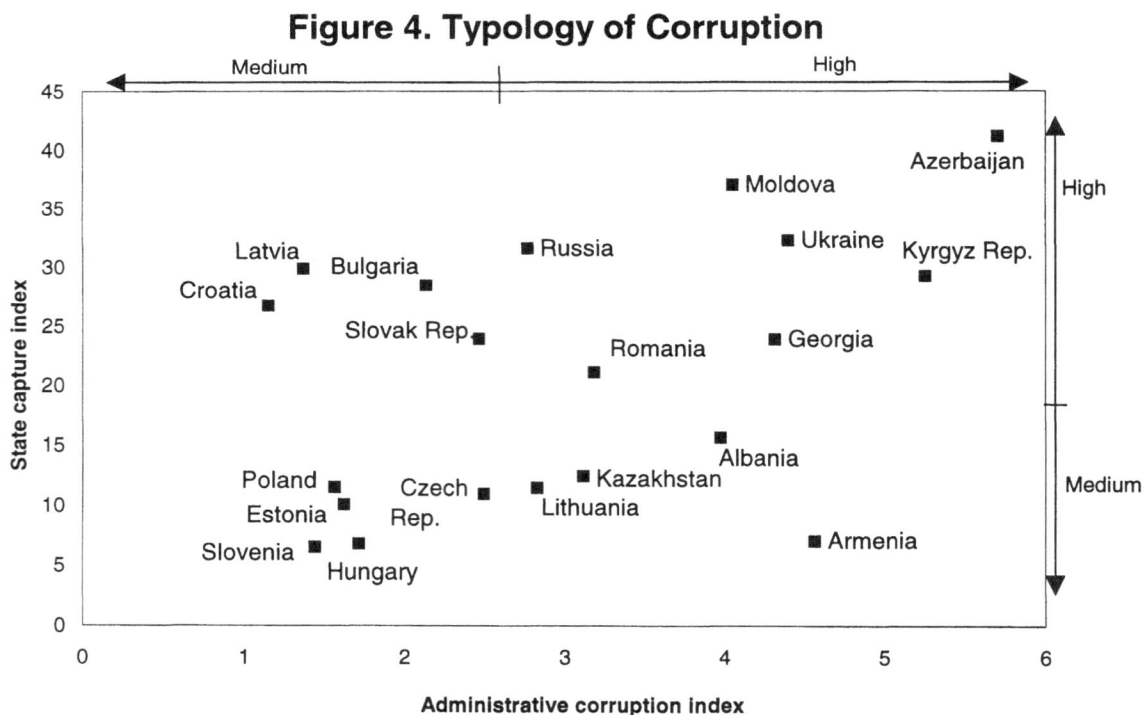

The typology is not intended to define absolute and unambiguous divisions among countries. Rather, it is presented as a heuristic device to highlight analytically and empirically the differences in patterns of corruption across countries. Like all aggregate indices, the measures of administrative corruption and state capture mask important variation across institutions within the state and across actors engaged in these activities. As a result, the typology cannot replace the critical role that individual country studies should play in identifying the extent and nature of the corruption problem and in further unbundling the forms of corruption identified in the report. Indeed, the typology should be seen more as a guide for self-assessment by countries as to the nature of the corruption problems they face, than as a definitive categorization of countries on these complex dimensions of corruption.

The typology can be divided into four spheres determined by the relative levels of state capture and administrative corruption:

- Countries within the **medium-medium** category have been able to contain both types of corruption to more manageable levels, though serious challenges remain.
- In the **medium-high** category are countries where the problem of administrative corruption remains the central problem, while the state has been less subject to capture by the private sector than other transition countries.
- The **high-medium** category includes countries that have been able to contain the level of administrative corruption relative to other transition countries, but nevertheless have done so in a context of high state capture.
- In the **high-high** category, a serious problem of administrative corruption—and hence, weak state capacity—is nested in a state highly subject to capture.

The typology presents a static picture of the pattern of corruption across transition countries at a single point in time, but it must be recognized that the pattern of corruption is much more dynamic. Indeed, in designing an effective anticorruption strategy, it might be more useful to know in which direction a country is moving within the typology rather than its position at any given time. The typology does not set out a simple linear path of development. Rather, countries can zigzag, progressing on one dimension of corruption, falling behind on the other, or moving ahead on both fronts simultaneously. Recognizing these different patterns and analyzing alternative evolutionary paths across these patterns could provide a stronger foundation for devising more appropriate and finely tuned anticorruption strategies in different contexts.

The Origins of Corruption in Transition

The simultaneous transition processes of building new political and economic institutions in the midst of a massive redistribution of state assets have created fertile ground for state capture and administrative corruption. Yet, there is tremendous variation across countries in both areas. An effective strategy for anticorruption must be based on an understanding of the root causes of different forms of corruption and their variation. Without it, policymakers run the risk of treating the symptoms without remedying the underlying conditions.

While it is impossible to disentangle with much certainty the complex interactions and lines of causality that determine variations in institutional outcomes across countries at any given point in time, it is possible to trace different paths of development over time. Countries entered the transition with very different initial conditions, i.e., levels of development, political and economic legacies, and natural and social endowments. These initial conditions influenced the early choices about the structure of political institutions and the nature of economic policies—choices that in turn affected alternative transition paths. The extent of state capture and administrative corruption is both a product of such transition paths and a driving force for further developments. However, the considerable variation in these forms of corruption both across and within geographic regions suggests the critical importance of political leadership, policy innovation and strategic vision in altering the course of transition.

As state capture is, by definition, a function of the concentration of economic power, differences in the structure of the economy across countries should have an impact on the potential for capture. In countries where national wealth is highly concentrated in a few key productive assets, there are significant risks that powerful interests will seek to gain control over them and invest some portion of their "windfall gains" to capture state institutions in an effort to sustain and strengthen their positions. Thus, countries richly endowed with natural resources (e.g., Azerbaijan, Russia, Kazakhstan, and Turkmenistan)

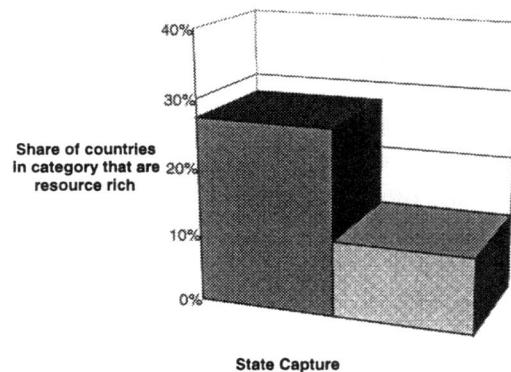

Figure 5. Resource Endowments and Corruption

or well placed to serve as transit routes for the distribution of these resources (e.g., Latvia) are prime candidates for state capture. Figure 5 makes clear that the level of state capture is higher in countries with greater endowments of natural resources.

The transition countries can be distinguished not only by their resource endowments but by the institutional legacies inherited from their pre-communist pasts. Some countries entered the transition with more highly developed systems of public administration and better trained public officials. For instance, countries with longer experience of sovereignty and closer links to European standards of civil service and judicial administration, as depicted in Figure 6, entered the transition with substantial advantages. These countries were also more likely to have adopted variants of market socialism during the communist period, which provided for a smaller role of the state in the economy and greater development of market institutions.

With a stronger legacy of sovereignty, these countries tended to develop more extensive social networks for collective action against the communist system when opportunities arose. As a result, the collapse of communism in these countries (for example in Hungary, Poland, and the Baltic states) was

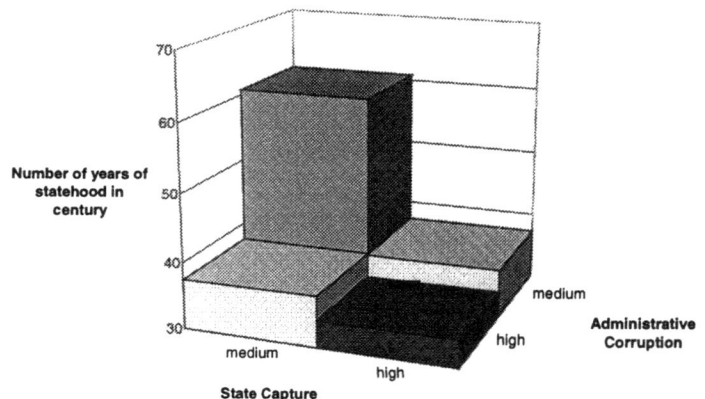

Figure 6. Statehood and Corruption

accompanied by social movements for change that generated a sharp break with previous political leaders and elites. This promoted greater political competition, the entry of new elites, and higher levels of accountability of these political leaders to the newly mobilized public.

In countries whose beneficial institutional legacies pushed them toward a transition path marked by a sharp break with the previous system, greater state capacity, and a civil society strong enough to promote change and accountability, we find a level and pace of political and economic reforms that have contained the worst excesses of corruption relative to other transition countries. State capture has been limited by stronger political competition and a civil society better able to constrain the power of concentrated economic interests. Administrative corruption has been limited by such a higher level of accountability, as well as by the more developed public institutions associated with a more advantageous historical legacy.

In contrast, countries that started the transition with greater continuity between the old and new systems, less developed public administrations, and weaker civil societies tended to adopt a path of partial political and economic reforms that intensified a wide range of rent-generating economic distortions and placed only minimal mechanisms for accountability on public officials. This has proven to be fertile ground for the growth of state capture and administrative corruption.

A Multi-pronged Strategy for Combating Corruption

The standard advice for combating corruption has traditionally focused on measures to address administrative corruption by reforming public administration and public finance management. But with the increasing recognition that the roots of corruption extend far beyond weaknesses in the capacity of government, the repertoire has been gradually expanding to target broader structural relationships, including the internal organization of the political system, relationships among core state institutions, the interactions between the state and firms, and the relationship between the state and civil society. An outline of this broader agenda is presented in Figure 7. Each block of this comprehensive set of instruments is designed to target a structural relationship that contributes to the level and profile of corruption.

Figure 7. Multi-pronged Strategy: Addressing State Capture and Administrative Corruption

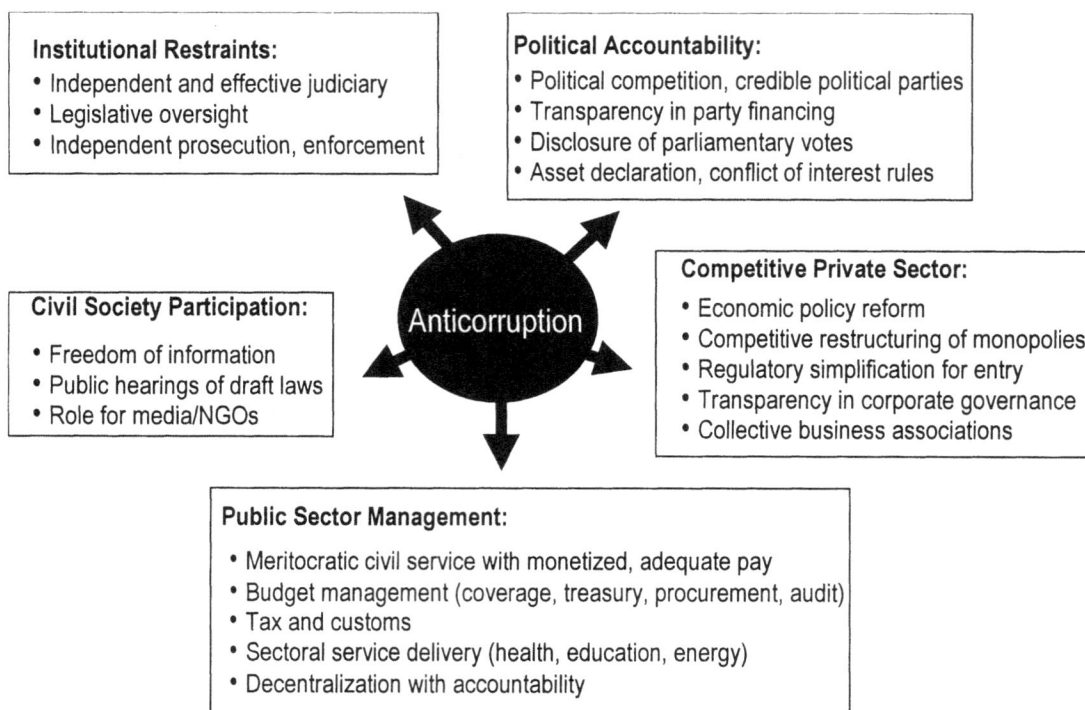

Institutional Restraints:
• Independent and effective judiciary
• Legislative oversight
• Independent prosecution, enforcement

Political Accountability:
• Political competition, credible political parties
• Transparency in party financing
• Disclosure of parliamentary votes
• Asset declaration, conflict of interest rules

Civil Society Participation:
• Freedom of information
• Public hearings of draft laws
• Role for media/NGOs

Anticorruption

Competitive Private Sector:
• Economic policy reform
• Competitive restructuring of monopolies
• Regulatory simplification for entry
• Transparency in corporate governance
• Collective business associations

Public Sector Management:
• Meritocratic civil service with monetized, adequate pay
• Budget management (coverage, treasury, procurement, audit)
• Tax and customs
• Sectoral service delivery (health, education, energy)
• Decentralization with accountability

Increasing political accountability: Political accountability refers to the constraints placed on the behavior of politicians and public officials by organizations and constituencies having the power to apply sanctions to them. As political accountability increases, the costs to politicians of making decisions that benefit their private interests at the expense of the broader public interest also increase. Two of the key instruments for strengthening political accountability are: (i) increasing the *transparency* of decisions made by public officials and (ii) increasing *competition* through organizations that provide broad constituencies with vehicles, such as mass-based political parties, for expressing their collective demands. Transparency can be fostered by a number of measures such as requiring public officials to disclose their income and assets to reveal conflict of interest. Such laws feature in many countries like Latvia, where the law penalizes illicit enrichment of officials who cannot justify possession of assets in excess of their normal source of income, and Lithuania, where the asset declaration law has been successfully used to remove corrupt officials from office.

Strengthening institutional restraints within the state: The institutional design of the state can be an important mechanism in checking corruption, in particular, the effective separation of powers among state entities with each operating as a check on the abuse of power by the others. Strengthening and raising the credibility of the judicial system by enhancing the independence and accountability of judges and matching functions with budget and capacity are particularly important. To hold governments accountable, parliaments need public accounts and audit committees, powers to require disclosure of government documents, and the capacity to implement credible sanctions. Audit organizations also play an important role. A good—but rare—example is Poland's Supreme Audit Chamber, which investigates and publishes reports on abuses in procurement, management of public assets, and other diversions of public funds. A condition for the effectiveness of these institutions is the establishment of a core of strong, credible, and independent professionals in the judicial, prosecutorial, and police arms of the state.

Strengthening civil society participation: As stakeholders in the quality of governance and as intermediaries for communication between the populace and the institutions of state, the organizations that comprise civil society can be essential in constraining corruption. Recently, there has been an emergence of greater civil society activism regarding corruption throughout the region, focused especially on: creating public awareness about corruption and the need to control it, formulating action plans to fight corruption, and monitoring government behavior. Civil society has proven to be most effective when the government treats it as a participatory ally. The experience of the Slovak Republic provides a good example: the national chapter of Transparency International was entrusted with the first draft of the National Program for the Fight Against Corruption and has regularly been invited to monitor procurements and other state decisions.

Fostering an independent media: Free and open media help check the level of corruption by uncovering and shedding light on abuses. Yet the promise of a free press has not yet been fully realized in many transition countries. Weakening the media's potentially powerful contribution to limiting corruption are: lingering state controls, conflicts of interest generated by ownership arrangements, and corruption in the media itself. A policy of openness, formalized in laws guaranteeing free access to information, strengthens tools for oversight and enlists the media as an ally in controlling corruption.

Creating a competitive private sector: A state is most vulnerable to capture when economic power is concentrated in a few firms or industries and when competing economic interests lack viable access to the policymaking process. The ability of powerful economic interests to capture the state can be checked by reducing the benefits to these firms from capture. This can be achieved in part by deepening price and trade liberalization, increasing transparency in the ownership structure and operations of firms, and introducing greater competition in concentrated sectors by lowering barriers to entry and requiring competitive restructuring. Reducing the ability of the state to extort bribes from the private sector requires deregulation. Hungary, Poland, and the Czech Republic have taken this approach, emphasizing the elimination of unnecessary licenses and rules and creating effective institutions for regulation. Both the potential for capture and the risk of administrative corruption can be diminished by strengthening instruments of voice, such as business associations, trade unions, and other collective actors for broad-based economic and social interests. A number of international conventions that aim to intensify the detection and punishment of transnational corruption, such as money laundering, are available for signature.

Reforming public sector management: While strengthening mechanisms of external accountability is important, it is also essential to strengthen the internal management of public resources and administration to reduce opportunities and incentives for corruption. This requires instilling meritocracy and adequate pay in public administration. Poland, Latvia, and Kazakhstan have made strides in this direction, initiating a meritocratic system for appointment, promotion, and performance evaluation. Moreover, changes in governance structures are needed to separate regulatory and economic functions and to rein in agencies outside policy and financial control. Transparency and accountability in fiscal management need to be enhanced by ensuring full budget coverage and control, instituting functioning budget planning and execution systems, and promoting the establishment of robust accounting and auditing. Opportunities for corruption in sectoral service delivery need to be reduced through policy reforms and greater public oversight. Finally, decentralization efforts need to focus on improving accountability and creating local capacity for financial management early in the process of decentralization.

Designing Effective Anticorruption Strategies

Taken together, the five building blocks of a multi-pronged approach to combating corruption might appear overwhelming, as they entail significant changes in the structure of existing economic and political institutions, in the nexus of relationships within the state and between state and society, and in the existing policy practices of governments. No government has the capacity to pursue simultaneous reforms in all of these areas. To be effective, a multi-pronged approach requires some guidelines for the selection and sequencing of reform priorities tailored to the particular contours of the corruption problem in each country. This report draws lessons from the typology to provide such guidelines.

Medium State Capture/Medium Administrative Corruption

Though the countries within this sphere exhibit lower levels of state capture and administrative corruption relative to other transition economies, the challenges are still significant. The political consequences of corruption are not necessarily correlated with the level of corruption. Where political competition is robust and the electorate increasingly sophisticated, complacency in the face of state capture and administrative corruption has the potential to generate even greater political instability than it does in less advanced, but more corrupt political systems.

Medium / Medium
Medium State Capture / Medium Administrative Corruption

Key Focus: Capitalizing on favorable conditions for strengthening political accountability and transparency through further institutional reforms

Challenges	*Priorities*
• Risk of complacency and backstepping • Close ties between economic interests and political institutions • Cronyism and conflict of interest in public sector appointments	• Promote further reforms in civil service, public finance, procurement, and judiciary • Introduce greater transparency into political financing • Develop strong partnerships with civil society

---

What distinguishes these countries is not the modesty of the corruption challenges they face, but the level of development of many of the key institutions and tools necessary to confront them. These include civil society institutions that are beginning to grow in strength, a vigorous independent media, an evolving system of institutional restraints within the state, functioning institutions of public administration, and some foundation for the rule of law. A good example is Poland, which has cross-party leadership, a vibrant media, and strong sources of advocacy and analysis from NGOs and academic institutes. Such institutions are necessary for building and empowering the domestic constituencies that generate sustained demand for combating corruption.

Most countries in this group continue to lack one or more of the following essential ingredients for an effective anticorruption strategy: i) political will; ii) collective action; and iii) relevant technical knowledge and practical experience.

Reducing state capture requires a strategy that goes beyond the classic technocratic approach. While relatively robust economic and political competition place some constraints on state capture in these countries, there are still vast areas open to abuse, in particular political party financing and conflicts of interest. Clear guidelines on financing political parties and mechanisms to enhance transparency are absolutely essential. The introduction—and effective implementation—of clear and comprehensive conflict of interest legislation could also have a powerful impact. Both areas require stronger verification and audit powers and further judicial and prosecutorial training and reform, worthy areas of institutional development in their own right. Strengthening enforcement mechanisms is also a feasible strategy in countries with a stronger framework for the rule of law.

At the same time, a high priority should be given to the implementation of best-practice technocratic reforms in the civil service, financial management and procurement, with the aim of increasing transparency, accountability, and efficiency in public administration and public finance. Committed political leadership of these reforms is essential.

Despite their many advantages, failure to act decisively to control state capture in these countries could run the risk of slipping backwards within the framework of the typology. The most likely path of regression in countries with reasonably stronger traditions of public administration is toward higher levels of state capture. As these economies grow, the capacity of powerful economic interests to influence fast-developing legal, legislative, and regulatory frameworks could outpace the constraints imposed by competing interest groups and civil society. The risk increases in those countries where a major agenda of structural reforms remains to be completed.

Medium State Capture/High Administrative Corruption

The main feature of most of the countries falling into this category—Albania provides an example—is the weak capacity of existing state institutions, both in terms of the provision of basic public goods and regulatory functions and the existing mechanisms of accountability and control within the state apparatus. Administrative corruption thrives in such an environment and often reaches the highest levels of the political system. State capture by firms is lower than in other transition countries. However, this does not appear to be due to any greater degree of political constraints on state actors, but rather to a less concentrated and less developed economic structure or to the overall lack of state capacity to intervene in the economy. There are also other forms of state capture, such as by public officials themselves or by specialized state sectors (e.g., the military) that may be relevant in individual cases, but are not measured in the BEEPS survey.

Medium / High
Medium State Capture / High Administrative Corruption

Key Focus: Enhancing state capacity to improve the provision of basic public goods.

Challenges
- Highly underdeveloped public administration
- Lack of control and accountability within the state
- Nascent civil society

Priorities
- Build the capacity of public administration
- Develop instruments for financial management
- Encourage civil society development

In such countries, anticorruption efforts should be synonymous with fundamental state-building. This entails, first and foremost, developing the capacity of the state to deliver basic public goods, such as public order and stability, health care and social protection, and simple systems of public revenue management. Enhancing the capacity of basic institutions of public administration and the civil service is necessary, but this should be combined with liberalizing measures to reduce bureaucratic discretion in the economy.

Civil society in these countries may be particularly weak; clans or other informal ties can lead to social fragmentation in some cases. Consequently, there are unlikely to be strong social constituencies to demand and sustain an anticorruption program. Public education and awareness are particularly critical elements of any anticorruption strategy in these countries, as the constituencies for reform within civil society are unlikely to have the capacity to sustain the demand side for anticorruption activities.

Perhaps one of the most serious problems in this group of countries is the looming threat of higher levels of state capture. As the private economy develops and gathers strength, there will be strong incentives for these actors to engage in state capture. Paradoxically, stability could carry greater risks of state capture by private firms, as the influence of other important constituencies within the state begins to subside.

High State Capture/Medium Administrative Corruption

Countries with high levels of state capture alongside medium levels of administrative corruption generally benefit from a historical legacy of the rule of law and well-developed public administrations associated with previous, pre-communist regimes. However, their problems with state capture can be rooted in either high concentrations of economic power in key industrial sectors or weakly accountable political regimes built around populist or nationalist politicians having close ties to powerful enterprises. An example of the first problem—high concentration of economic power—is Latvia, where political parties are closely aligned with economic interests, and its geographical location on east-west trade and energy transit routes exposes it to strong corruption pressure. The second problem—weakly accountable political regimes—was the case with the first governments after independence in Croatia and the Slovak Republic. State capture can be seen as repressing the advantages that these countries have in terms of the capacity of the state and the strength of public administration.

High / Medium
High State Capture / Medium Administrative Corruption

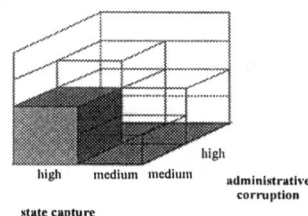

Key Focus: Enhancing political accountability and promoting new entry to take maximum advantage of a stronger legacy of state capacity.

Challenges	Priorities
• High concentration of power by vested interests	• Broaden formal channels of access to the state
• Weak structures for monitoring and accountability	• Deconcentrate economic power through competition and entry
• Powerful groups block further reforms to preserve their advantages	• Enhance oversight through participatory strategies

---

The major obstacles to further progress on structural reform lie less in the weak capacity of state institutions than in the power of vested economic interests and the private interests of powerful politicians. Though basic political institutions and civil society are much more developed in this group compared with the previous one, mechanisms of political accountability tend to be attenuated due, in some instances, to the semi-authoritarian nature of the political regimes. Conflicts of interest abound as political strongmen tend to equate their private well-being with the country's well-being. Favored firms develop close ties to political leaders and their parties, often blurring the boundaries between the party and the firm.

Though technocratic reforms might be useful as entry points into anticorruption work, a credible reform program should be designed to broaden formal channels of political access and to increase the accountability of public officials to a wider range of constituencies. Efforts to promote collective action among anticorruption constituencies and competing interest groups should play an important role in an anticorruption strategy. Encouraging the development of institutional mechanisms of political oversight and promoting transparency in party financing could also have a positive impact. In sequencing an anticorruption strategy, the early promotion of political reforms and partnerships with civil society has the potential to achieve a considerable impact.

It is in this group of countries that a democratic change of regime can offer the greatest opportunities for implementing a comprehensive anticorruption strategy. Regime change is sometimes accompanied by a resurgence of political competition, a strengthening of political parties, and a rejuvenation of civil society that can increase accountability pressures on the new leadership. This could create a valuable window of opportunity to promote an anticorruption strategy that strikes at the root causes of the problem. Such a window of opportunity is evident in the Slovak Republic, where the coalition elected in 1998 has put anticorruption high on the agenda and there are some indications that perceived levels of corruption, though still high, have fallen.

Failure to constrain and reduce state capture could lead to further regression and the erosion of existing state capacity that keeps administrative corruption in check. The prolonged use of corrupt incentives to influence policymakers and administrators leads to diminishing confidence in public servants and state institutions. Informal networks are strengthened to gain access to privilege. Growing informality weakens revenue collection, limiting the resources available to maintain a professional civil service and support public finances.

High State Capture/High Administrative Corruption

Finally, there are countries where state institutions with weak administrative capacity coexist with a high concentration of vested interests and a state highly susceptible to capture. In these cases, the challenge of combating corruption is particularly difficult. Powerful private interests have the capacity to block institutional reforms that would limit their capacity to extract rents from the state and eliminate market distortions that work to their advantage. The government lacks sufficient mechanisms of control and accountability throughout the state bureaucracy to implement institutional and policy reforms. Nascent civil societies and intermediary associations do not have sufficient power to counterbalance the weight of concentrated vested interests. This is the most difficult environment in which to design an effective anticorruption program.

High / High
High State Capture / High Administrative Corruption

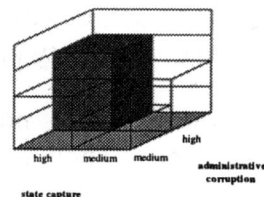

Key Focus: Breaking the hold of vested interests on the policymaking process

Challenges	*Priorities*
• Highly concentrated economic interests	• Deconcentrate economic interests through restructuring, competition and enhanced entry
• Limited implementation capacity of government	• Build accountability and oversight mechanisms
• Weak anticorruption constituencies	• Promote collective action among countervailing interests
• Restricted channels of access for countervailing interests	• Stand-alone technocratic reforms will have limited impact

Stand-alone efforts to tackle administrative corruption through technocratic reforms in public administration and public finance are likely to have limited impact. The institutional context is as yet too weak to deliver the minimum necessary underpinnings for reform. Given the low level of organization of civil society and constricted formal channels of interest intermediation for countervailing social groups, such efforts are unlikely to prove sustainable over time.

Targeting state capture requires measures on two fronts: (i) decreasing the gains to "captor" firms deriving from state capture and (ii) increasing the costs to politicians of state capture. Decreasing the gains to captors entails deconcentrating vested economic interests through competitive restructuring of monopolies, reducing barriers to entry, and increasing transparency in corporate governance. Increasing the costs to politicians requires efforts to foster collective action among potential countervailing interests, such as "second-tier" companies and small- and medium-sized enterprises, to obtain political access. This could entail the development of business and trade associations and formal lobby groups to increase the range of interests with access to government, to foster competition in an effort to reduce the concentration of existing rent streams, and to strengthen formal and transparent channels of political influence. The goal is to promote a greater number and diversity of economic actors competing through more transparent and open conduits of political access for a limited pool of rents.

On the costs to politicians, the weak organization of civil society and low level of accountability and transparency within the state suggest that efforts should begin with building credible constituencies in and outside the government to bring the very issue of corruption to the forefront. Without such constituencies, serious institutional reforms to enhance accountability and to strengthen civil society participation are unlikely to have a sustainable impact.

Expectations should not be unrealistic and the time horizon of reform should be considered quite long. Though occasional windows of opportunity for reform might arise, it is crucial to recognize that the extent of state capture, the concentration of economic interests, and the institutional weaknesses of the state will serve as powerful constraints on the effectiveness and sustainability of reforms introduced through such windows. Anticorruption assistance programs should be designed around achievable "litmus tests" to gauge the government's commitment to reform and to recognize the limitations in such environments. Efforts to build up demonstration effects through intensive work with carefully selected organizations, sectors, or regional authorities might provide a method of entry into broader anticorruption work.

Operationalizing an Anticorruption Strategy

Though the typology provides a framework for tailoring individual anticorruption strategies in different contexts, there are a number of cross-cutting principles that can be essential in operationalizing an effective strategy. They provide a framework for gaining a foothold to begin anticorruption work, building credibility behind an anticorruption strategy, and enhancing the sustainability of that strategy over time.

Credible political leadership: A serious anticorruption program cannot be imposed from the outside, but requires committed leadership from within, ideally from the highest levels of the state. While pressure for reform can come from below—indeed, this can effectively generate a needed social consensus—any effective program must be supported from the top.

Diagnosing the nature and extent of the problem in each case: Implementing surveys, running workshops, and developing a dialogue with institutions of civil society on corruption are all critical for gaining country-specific knowledge beyond the narrow limits of the typology. The process can also play a major role in building anticorruption constituencies.

Assessing the environment: The relevance and feasibility of specific reform instruments is closely linked to the way in which power is exercised, the level of informality in the society, and the extent to which people feel trust in their institutions and in each other. These factors create an enabling or constraining environment, together with incentives and disincentives for change, that must be taken into account in the choice and sequencing of instruments if anticorruption strategies are to be realistic and effective.

Finding appropriate entry points: It is critical to begin at a point where the goals are feasible and tangible results can be realized within a time frame that builds support for further reforms. Small gains can provide essential levers to sway public and official opinion.

Maximizing leverage: Efforts should be made to design "win-win" anticorruption strategies that promote the interests and reputations of major politicians and businesspeople while delivering positive externalities such as enhancing economic growth, strengthening governance, or reducing poverty and inequality.

Conclusion

The challenge ahead for transition countries is to strengthen the commitment to tackle corruption. The task will not be easy. The status quo often benefits powerful interests, state capture poses formidable challenges, and the political economy of anticorruption initiatives has proven complex and difficult. The roots of these problems reach deep into historical legacies, economic structures, and transition paths. While valuable windows of opportunity may arise in specific countries, it remains important to manage expectations and underscore the long-term nature of reform, while still taking decisive actions and building credibility.

Reform and progress are possible and the costs of doing nothing are extremely high. Unbundling corruption and tailoring reform strategies to target the specific profile of the problem in different countries provide important insights into the design of effective anticorruption strategies. After ten years of transition, the building blocks of reform are now better known, but the challenge remains to prioritize and sequence these reforms in a manner that can build credible support for a sustainable process of change. By analyzing the factors underlying the *persistence* of corruption in different contexts, this report provides a framework for meeting this challenge.

Chapter 1: The Level and Pattern of Corruption in the Transition Countries

In recent years, a consensus has emerged across the globe on the high costs of corruption for economic, political, and social development. There has also been broad agreement on an approach to combating corruption that focuses on limiting the *discretionary* powers of state officials to intervene in the economy.[1] As a result, the fight against corruption in the transition countries has been incorporated into a wider reform agenda combining liberalization and privatization to roll back the state and governance reforms to promote greater transparency and accountability in the state's legal and regulatory framework. However, the experience of the first decade of transition in reducing corruption has been decidedly mixed. Efforts to reform basic state institutions have generally had limited impact. Anticorruption campaigns have been hijacked for narrow political advantage. Governance reforms have frequently been blocked by powerful vested interests. The political will to implement and sustain structural reforms has often been lacking. This experience suggests that, although we may know a great deal about the causes and consequences of corruption, we know much less about the factors underlying the *persistence* of corruption.

Part of the problem comes from unrealistic expectations about the time necessary to address the fundamental roots of corruption, even in the fast-paced environment of the transition. But an important part of the problem also lies in the tendency to focus exclusively on the state and, in so doing, to limit our anticorruption strategy to standardized technical solutions. This has led to an incomplete and overly uniform approach to combating corruption that does not take into account important differences among countries in the capacity of the state, the power and concentration of economic interests, and the channels of accountability between the state and civil society—all of which are crucial determinants of the pattern and persistence of corruption across countries.

This report attempts to develop a more nuanced approach to corruption. It begins by unbundling the problem to recognize that different dimensions of corruption might have unique origins and consequences.[2] On this basis, a typology of corruption is developed to distinguish among different patterns of the problem across the transition countries. Specific policy recommendations are tailored to these distinct patterns, drawing from a common set of institutional and policy reforms, and with emphasis on how to target anticorruption efforts, how to sequence reforms, and how to calibrate realistic expectations in different contexts.

The typology is based on the distinction between two types of corruption—*state capture* and *administrative corruption*. State capture refers to the actions of individuals, groups, or firms in both the public and private sectors *to influence the formation* of laws, regulations, decrees, and other government policies (i.e., the basic rules of the game) to their own advantage by means of the illicit and non-transparent provision private benefits to public officials (see Box 1.1 for a further discussion of this concept). For example, an influential "oligarch" at the head of a powerful financial-industrial group could buy off legislators to erect barriers to entry in a particular sector. Alternatively, the state can be captured to serve the private interests of a political leader who shapes the framework of reforms to ensure his own private control over key resources.

There are many different forms of state capture. Distinctions can be drawn between the types of institutions that are captured—the legislature, the executive, the judiciary, or regulatory agencies. Further distinctions can be made on the basis of who does the capturing—private firms, political leaders, or narrow interest groups. One could even distinguish between the nature of the benefits provided to public officials in exchange for capture—direct bribes, illicit equity stakes, informal control rights. Yet all forms of state capture are directed toward extracting rents from the state for a narrow range of individuals, firms, or sectors through distorting the basic legal and regulatory framework, with potentially enormous losses for the society at large. They thrive where economic power is highly concentrated, countervailing social interests are weak, and the formal channels of political influence and interest intermediation are underdeveloped.

While state capture encodes advantages for particular individuals or groups in the basic legal or regulatory framework, administrative corruption refers to the intentional imposition of distortions in the prescribed *implementation* of existing laws, rules, and regulations to provide advantages to either state or non-state actors as a result of the illicit and non-transparent provision of private gains to public officials. The classic example of administrative corruption is that of a hapless shop owner forced to pay bribes to a seemingly endless stream of official inspectors to overlook minor (or possibly major) infractions of existing regulations. Beyond such forms of extortion, administrative corruption also includes such familiar examples of "grease payments" as bribes to gain licenses, to smooth customs procedures, to win public procurement contracts, or to be given priority in the provision of a variety of other government services. Finally, state officials can simply misdirect public funds under their control for their own or their family's direct financial benefit. At the root of this form of corruption is discretion on the part of public officials to grant selective exemptions, to prioritize the delivery of public services, or to discriminate in the application of rules and regulations.

Both state capture and administrative corruption can cut across different levels of government.[3] Both can be initiated by state officials, private businessmen, or other non-state actors. The key difference is neither who extracts the rents nor how important is the official who receives the bribe, but rather the nature of the political relationship underlying each form of corruption. In capturing the state, actors prejudice the rules to their own narrow advantage, which subsequently constrains the actions of others in the economy. Through administrative corruption, actors obtain individualized exceptions to or favorable application of those rules. The difference lies in how deep the corrupt transaction reaches into the operations and functions of the state and the extent to which the advantages of the corrupt transaction are institutionalized into the basic rules of the game. Though there will be many specific cases where the borderline dividing these two forms of corruption might be difficult to draw with a high degree of certainty, the distinction nevertheless has important analytical and practical implications for the potential effectiveness of different anticorruption strategies.

Box 1.1: The Concept of State Capture

The definition of state capture used in this report is derived from the concept of regulatory capture, already well established in the economics literature.[4] State regulatory agencies are said to be "captured" when they regulate businesses in accordance with the private interests of the regulated as opposed to the public interest for which they were established. Though regulatory capture can occur through the provision of private gains, both direct and indirect, by regulated businesses to state officials, it is not limited to influence through corrupt means.[5]

State capture is a broader concept in that it encompasses the formation of laws, rules, and decrees by a wider range of state institutions, including the executive, ministries and state agencies, legislature, and the judiciary. At the same time, state capture has a narrower definition in that it focuses exclusively on illicit, illegitimate and non-transparent forms of influence.

Who can capture the state? Often, the "captors" are individuals, groups, or firms from the private sector seeking rents or other advantages from the state. Yet any actors with access to public officials and the capacity to provide private benefits to these officials in order to obtain advantages in the governing process can be seen as potential captors. Indeed, public officials themselves can capture the state if they abuse their authority to shape institutions and laws primarily to further their own private financial interests at the expense of the broader public interest, though identifying and indeed measuring such conflicts of interest are nearly impossible in the context of the transition.

The influence of private interests on the decisions of the state is a normal feature of all political systems. What separates state capture as a form of corruption from conventional forms of political influence, such as lobbying, are the mechanisms by which the private interests interact with the state. State capture occurs through the illicit provision of private gains to public officials via informal, nontransparent, and highly preferential channels of access. It can also occur through unclear boundaries between the political and business interests of state officials, which has been a particularly prominent characteristic of many transition countries. In all its forms, state capture tends to subvert, or even replace, legitimate and transparent channels of political influence and interest intermediation, reducing the access of competing groups and interests to state officials.

Different forms of state capture as distinguished by different types of captors (e.g., private firms, politicians, ethnic groups, the military) and different state institutions involved (e.g., the executive branch, the legislature, the judiciary, or regulatory bodies) will undoubtedly have their own unique dynamics and consequences. Therefore, state capture itself could be unbundled to reveal a wide range of different relationships.

Reducing state capture does not entail eliminating private sector influence on the formation of policies, rules, and laws by the state. Indeed, such influence can be an important factor pushing forward both economic and political reform. Nor will it be resolved by legalizing private payments to public officials. Rather, reducing state capture involves shifting private sector influence from illicit, nontransparent, and highly preferential channels of access toward legitimate, transparent, and competitive forms of interest intermediation. It also involves developing clearer boundaries between the political and business roles of state officials in order to prevent conflicts of interest.

Though the report highlights the problem of state capture in transition countries, it is by no means confined to the transition and continues to be a serious problem in most societies. Yet the problem in many transition countries is exacerbated by the high concentration of economic power, the poorly developed formal channels of political influence and interest intermediation, and the weak organization of countervailing interests both from the economy and civil society.

In analyzing different forms of corruption, this report places primary emphasis on the interaction between the state and the private sector. Of course, this dimension represents only one subset of corruption. Corrupt transactions can occur entirely within the state, for example when politicians bribe bureaucrats. The misuse of public authority for private gain need not require the participation of private sector actors.[6] At the same time, corruption within the private sector itself can be an important dimension of the problem. Asset-stripping, abuse of minority shareholder rights, and bribery to obtain private services in restricted or distorted markets are all forms of corruption that do not directly involve public officials (though their indirect complicity is often an important factor). While these forms of "public-to-public" and "private-to-private" corruption will be discussed in the report, the focus on the interaction between the state and the private sector is rooted in the particular nature of the process of transition, characterized by the simultaneous building of the state and the market economy.

Faced with the concurrent challenges of defining the basic rules of the game, redistributing the bulk of state assets, forming new political structures, and establishing the key institutions of a market economy, most transition countries have been unable to define clear boundaries and effective forms of intermediation between the state and the private sector. The fusion of the party and the command economy that characterized the previous communist system has been replaced in many countries of the region by a new fusion of the transitional state and the now largely private economy. Political leaders are closely tied to business empires. Political parties are thinly veiled fronts for powerful firms. The media trumpet the rival interests of oligarchs to explain key policy decisions of the state. Though such phenomena are hardly unique to transition, the simultaneity of the political and economic transformations in a highly truncated time frame has exacerbated the opportunities for state capture in the transition countries.

Yet despite its importance, the lack of reliable empirical data on state capture has prevented serious empirical investigation. This report presents and analyses the first systematic data on state capture collected in the transition economies, along with new efforts to quantify the level and impact of administrative corruption. The data come from the 1999 Business Environment and Enterprise Performance Survey (BEEPS), a firm-level survey commissioned jointly by the World Bank and the European Bank for Reconstruction and Development (EBRD) to assess obstacles in the business environment across the transition economies (see Box 1.2 for a description of the survey).[7] Based on more than 3,000 interviews with the owners and senior managers of firms in 22 countries across the region, the BEEPS data provide an opportunity to investigate state capture and administrative corruption from the point of view of some of those most directly affected. While the BEEPS data spotlight the relations between the state and firms, data from a wealth of audit reports, empirical studies, and detailed diagnostic surveys in selected transition countries are also presented to provide a broader picture of other forms of corruption from the perspectives of households and state officials. These surveys constitute a major step forward in understanding the depth and contours of the problem of corruption within and across countries.

Box 1.2: The Business Environment and Enterprise Performance Survey

The BEEPS survey was conducted on the basis of face-to-face interviews with firm managers or owners in site visits during the period June through August 1999 in the following countries: Albania, Armenia, Azerbaijan, Belarus, Bulgaria, Croatia, Czech Republic, Estonia, Georgia, Hungary, Kazakhstan, Kyrgyz Republic, Latvia, Lithuania, Moldova, Poland, Romania, the Russian Federation, Slovak Republic, Slovenia, Ukraine, and Uzbekistan. With the exception of Albania and Latvia, the survey was conducted in all countries by local staff of an international survey firm to ensure consistency of training and approach across countries.

In each country, between 125 and 150 firms were interviewed, with the exception of three countries where larger samples were used: Poland (250), Russia (550), and Ukraine (250). The sample was structured to be fairly representative of the domestic economies with specific quotas placed on size, sector, location, and export orientation. The sample was heavily weighted toward privately owned firms, though there were quotas for state-owned firms and firms with foreign ownership. However, no attempt was made to construct a representative sample across these ownership strata and the quotas were designed only to ensure representation.

Attempts to compare levels of corruption across different countries are fraught with difficulties. Most existing cross-country surveys of governance and corruption rely on the subjective views of outsiders, namely expert assessments, country analysts, or foreign investors.[8] The results of such surveys are thus highly subjective and estimated with a large margin of error that inhibits cross-country comparisons.[9] The BEEPS relies on the direct experience of firms rather than external subjective comparisons across countries. Where possible, numerical cardinal estimates of problems are used (such as share of annual revenue spent on bribes) to measure the extent of the problem, as well as to gauge the specific costs and benefits to the firm associated with corruption. These estimates enable us to measure the margin of error on many questions, which are reported in the form of error bars in the figures below.

As many of the forms of corruption examined in this report are illegal in most countries, firms must be expected to be reluctant to admit that they engage in such activity. In implementing the survey, the problems associated with collecting reliable data were kept constantly in mind, and every effort was made to assure respondents that their answers would be treated confidentially. Questions were phrased indirectly about the corruption faced by "firms in your line of business" and respondents were assured that responses would be aggregated and not attributable to themselves or their firms. The survey questions examine corruption from a number of different angles, providing consistency checks on each firm's responses. Moreover, tests were conducted to detect any systematic positive or negative bias among the firms in any given country. The ranking of transition countries on the indices of administrative corruption and state capture used in this report remain basically unchanged when individual firm characteristics such as size, sector, and ownership are controlled for statistically.

Source: Hellman, Jones, Kaufmann, and Schankermann (2000).

The report is divided into six chapters. This chapter goes on to investigate the incidence and pattern of corruption in the transition countries, developing a country typology of corruption that frames the entire report. Chapter Two examines the consequences and costs of different forms of corruption on economic performance, poverty and inequality, and the credibility of the state. Chapter Three looks into the origins of these different patterns of corruption, tracing alternative paths of transition and how they are shaped by initial conditions, institutional structures, and policy choices. Chapters Four and Five present the policy recommendations for combating corruption that have been derived from the analysis. The former sets out the building blocks to design an anticorruption strategy, while the latter draws lessons for combining, prioritizing, and sequencing these building blocks to address most effectively the particular contours of the challenge of corruption in different countries. Chapter Six draws conclusions on the basis of existing international experience.

The Extent of Corruption in the Transition Countries

According to most existing efforts to compare perceptions of the level of corruption across countries, many of the transition economies—in particular in the CIS—are seen to have among the highest corruption indicators of all the countries surveyed. According to a summary index developed from a weighted average of 12 of the most widely known cross-country corruption indices with data from 1996-1999, the level of corruption in the CIS countries is perceived to be comparable with the levels in South Asia and Sub-Saharan Africa as depicted in Figure 1.1.[10] In contrast, corruption in Central and Eastern Europe and the Baltics is seen to be on par with Latin America and the Middle East, though the level remains considerably higher than it is in the Organisation for Economic Co-operation and Development (OECD) countries.

Figure 1.1. World-wide Perceptions of Corruption

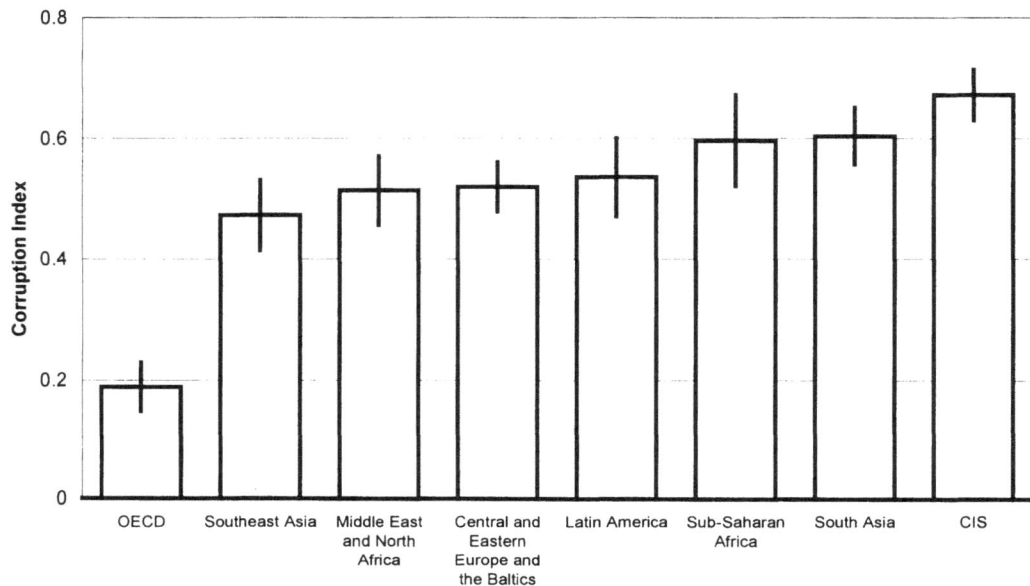

The thin line at the top of each bar represents the statistical margin of error (based on a single standard deviation) calculated on the basis of the aggregated indicators. Source: Kaufmann, Kraay, and Zoido-Lobaton (1999a).

While such comparisons are a useful indicator of international *perceptions* of corruption, they provide little assistance in developing effective anticorruption strategies. They tend to be based on the perceptions of external observers and investors rather than those of nationals having direct experience of corruption in these countries. They collapse many different forms of corruption into a single scale without recognizing the diverse patterns of corruption that can be found in many countries. They hide important variation in the nature and level of corruption within regions in any individual country. Enhancing the measurement and analysis of this variation can provide critical insights both into the nature of corruption and the development of strategies to combat the problem.

Unbundling Corruption in Transition

The BEEPS survey unbundles corruption to examine state capture and administrative corruption separately to provide an empirical foundation for a more complex analysis of the pattern of corruption in each country. However, the BEEPS data do not provide a comprehensive measure of corruption in the transition countries. The survey focuses on the forms of corruption in the enterprise sector that are subject to reliable measurement. As a result, the questions tend to be biased toward those corrupt transactions in which direct payments are made to public officials by enterprises. This leaves out a very wide range of corrupt transactions in which other forms of benefits that are much more difficult to identify and measure are transferred to public officials, for example, equity stakes in firms, gifts and services, or promises of future benefits. In particular, the critical issue of conflicts of interest among public officials is not addressed in the survey, as the boundaries between politics and business are inherently difficult to identify, much less to measure across countries. It is likely that these different manifestations of corrupt transactions are all highly correlated, though this remains an issue for further study.[11]

In addition, the BEEPS survey provides a measure of corruption only from the perspective of the firm in relation to its interactions with the state. Consequently, the data do not capture a wide range of corrupt transactions that occur between public officials, between private sector actors, or between individuals and the state. In some transition countries, pure public finance corruption (i.e., theft or misappropriation of funds without the participation of firms) is likely to be even more important than the public-private nexus. To supplement the BEEPS data, we rely on surveys of households and public officials that were conducted in the context of "diagnostic exercises" on corruption in selected countries of the region. Country examples are also used to highlight forms of corruption that are particularly difficult to measure and compare across countries.

Measuring Administrative Corruption

On the basis of the BEEPS data, indicators of the level of administrative corruption can be constructed and compared across countries. As a proxy for a wide range of manifestations of administrative corruption, firms were asked to estimate the share of their revenues that they typically pay per annum in unofficial payments to public officials in order to influence the implementation of state policies, regulations, and laws in each country.[12] Figure 1.2 presents the results aggregated by country.

Figure 1.2. Administrative Corruption *(bribes as a share of annual revenues)*

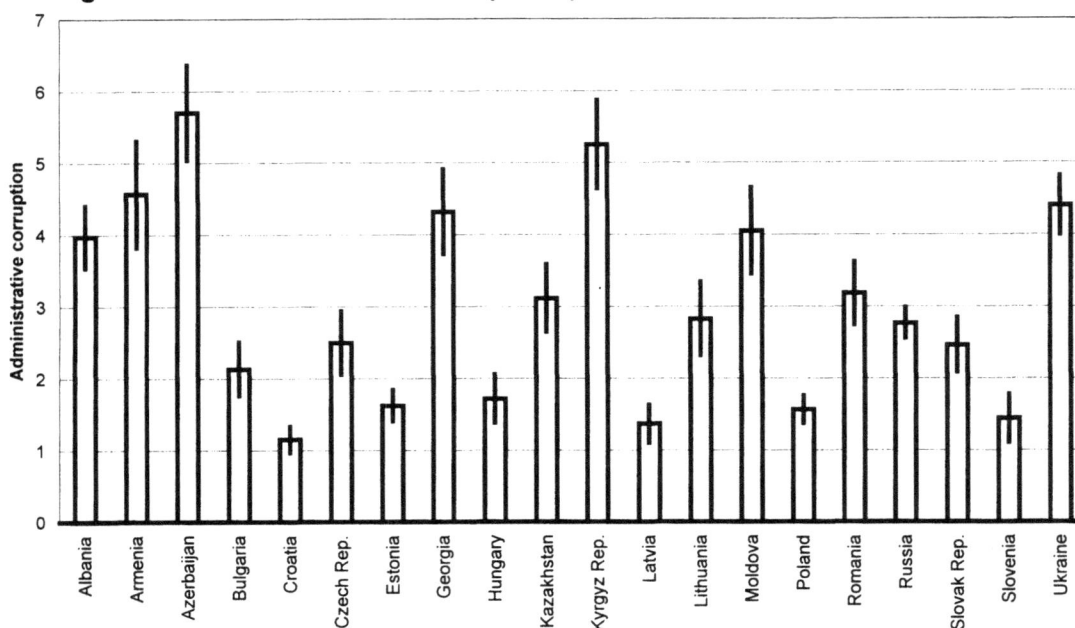

The thin line at the top of each bar represents the statistical margin of error (based on a single standard deviation) calculated for each country within the sample. Source: BEEPS.

Across the countries of the CIS, average payments for administrative corruption are estimated by firms to be 3.7 percent of their annual revenues; the share falls to 2.2 percent of revenues in Central and Eastern Europe.[13] Yet measuring administrative corruption as a share of firm revenues does not convey the full weight of the burden of this form of corruption. Though data on profit margins for firms in transition economies are notoriously unreliable, given the strong incentives to conceal profits and operate in the unofficial economy, the BEEPS survey does provide a rough estimate of profit margins for firms that can be used to give a very crude estimate of administrative corruption as a share of profits. Using the average reported profit margin of 22 percent in the CIS countries and 13 percent in Central and Eastern Europe (CEE), administrative corruption constitutes approximately 17 percent of profits across the region. Though such estimates should be treated with considerable caution, they provide an indication of the heavy burden of administrative corruption on firms in transition countries.

Beyond the clear differences between the CIS and CEE, the variation in administrative corruption across countries within these regions is substantial. Some countries within CEE, such as Albania and Romania, have reported levels of administrative corruption on par with the CIS countries. Within the CIS, the highest levels of administrative corruption are reported in the Caucasus, Kyrgyz Republic, and Ukraine. Other CIS countries fall within ranges more comparable to countries in CEE.

The most commonly reported form of administrative corruption is unofficial payments to obtain licenses and permits from the state. Other common forms of administrative corruption include payments to deal with taxes and tax collection and to gain government contracts. A more comprehensive picture of the extent of administrative corruption in transition countries can be gained from household surveys, since individuals can also make unofficial payments to alter the implementation of government policies. Household surveys in selected transition countries show that corruption within the police force, particularly the traffic police, and the health services accounts for approximately half of all bribe payments by households.[14] Bribe payments associated with the educational system, especially at higher levels of the system, are also relatively common.

Measuring State Capture

Measuring the extent of state capture across countries presents a number of challenges. First, relying on the BEEPS firm level data, we can only attempt to measure the extent to which *firms* have managed to influence various state institutions in any given country. Other forms of state capture that do not include private sector participation, such as capture by politicians for their own private interests or by other non-state individuals and groups cannot be examined through a firm level survey. As a result, measures based on the BEEPS data understate the overall level of state capture in any country, while providing a more accurate measure of state capture by private and public firms. This underestimation of overall state capture may be particularly high in countries with kleptocratic political regimes, where institutions of the state have been used to serve the interests of a particular leader and his broader circle (for further discussion of the important issue of "who captures whom" see Box 1.3).

Box 1.3: Who Captures Whom?

State capture can clearly take many forms beyond the purchase of laws and decrees by private and public enterprises. State officials may use their positions to capture enterprises, or may channel state funds for their personal use in ways that do not involve other players at all. Yet the salient feature of these forms of capture is the same as that of enterprise-state capture: the perversion of the rules of the game, through corruption, to the benefit of the captors, rather than for society as a whole.

State capture can also be undertaken by actors within state institutions—the parliament, the executive, or the judiciary. Ministers may shape laws, regulations, or tax policy to benefit themselves or their own financial interests. In a number of countries ruling groups have disposed of assets for privatization through closed mechanisms designed to preclude competition and to benefit themselves or their associates, enabling them to gain control of substantial parts of the economy. In state-initiated capture, an explicit transaction need not take place, though there may be an implicit contract or expectation of future rewards through *quid pro quo* asset transfers or employment in advantageous posts. The defining characteristic is that representatives of state power, whether in the legislature, executive, or judiciary, manipulate state powers for their own private gain.

The terrain for this kind of capture is larger when a substantial part of the economy remains in state hands. Appointments to boards of state-owned enterprises can be a license to make money out of diversion of products, or closed procurement, including setting up contracts with companies owned by the board members. In these cases, the gains may be shared beyond the individuals who engineer them, with some part of the bribes and other advantages being channeled back to the political party that ensured the appointment to the lucrative post.

One key source of the problem is that the concept of a conflict between public duties and private interests is either poorly understood or inadequately respected. Safeguards against conflict of interest are key, and it is noteworthy that many countries of the region have adopted legislation designed to prevent parliamentarians and other officials from acting in a situation of conflict of interest. While few countries have implemented this legislation effectively, its existence is a signal of aspirations to restrict state capture emanating from within the state.

Second, the dynamics of state capture may be very different depending on the extent and nature of the private sector in any given country. Where the economy is still largely dominated by state ownership and key elements of the command system continue to function, the capacity of the nascent private sector to capture the state will be minimal. Indeed, the very dynamics of state capture might be expected to differ in countries where some minimal threshold of private sector development has not been crossed. As a result, though the BEEPS survey was implemented in some countries where such a threshold has yet to be reached—namely, Belarus and Uzbekistan—the results are discussed separately in order to recognize the unique nature of the problem in these cases (see Box 1.4).[15]

Box 1.4: Corruption When Transition is Stalled

A number of former Soviet republics (including Belarus, Uzbekistan, and Turkmenistan) have made very limited progress towards either a market economy or a multiparty political system. These countries retain substantial similarities with key elements of the previous command administrative system.

In these countries the private sector has a small share in GDP and employment (20 percent in Belarus, 25 percent in Turkmenistan, and 45 percent in Uzbekistan, where in agriculture it may by grossly over-estimated) and is subject to strict bureaucratic controls, state orders and lack of credit. There are still large scale price controls with widespread subsidies and occasional shortages. Industrial policy is product- and enterprise-oriented; central commands still abound. Multiple exchange rates, with overvalued official rates and undervalued parallel rates, are distortionary and lead to low trade flows and high current account deficits. FDI levels have remained extremely low. The EBRD's transition indicators rank Belarus, Turkmenistan, and Uzbekistan lowest among all the transition economies.*

According to international perceptions, the level of corruption in these countries is quite high. Belarus is ranked 58th of 99 countries surveyed in the Corruption Perceptions Index by Transparency International, while Uzbekistan is ranked 94th (Turkmenistan is not assessed). Yet according to the BEEPS survey, the percentage of firms impacted by state capture in these countries is reported to be among the lowest in the region, as reported below. Though there is much greater variation in the extent of administrative corruption, one of the slowest reformers – Belarus – also records one of the lowest levels of this form of corruption. Does this suggest that highly authoritarian regimes are more effective at preventing administrative corruption and state capture than democratic systems?

	Administrative Corruption (bribes as a share of revenues)	State Capture (percent of firms affected by state capture)
Belarus	1.3	8.0
Uzbekistan	4.4	5.8

Source: BEEPS. See Figures 1.2 and 1.3 to put these numbers in perspective.

The answer lies in the nature of the BEEPS survey. The BEEPS data measure corruption by firms, primarily in the private sector. Thus, state capture, as measured in this report, assumes the development of some degree of autonomy between the state and the private sector. Where the private sector is barely developed and the state continues to own and control most of the economy through administrative methods, this autonomy does not exist. In such an environment, the BEEPS questions on state capture may not provide an adequate depiction of the relationship between the state and firms.

When an authoritarian regime continues to exercise considerable control over both the executive and the judiciary, administrative corruption may be kept in check. Although such scenarios could lead to relatively low levels of capture and administrative corruption as empirically measured by the survey, this implies that the transition is still in its infancy. Hence the lower incidence of corruption in Belarus is likely to reflect lack of reform in the guise of a small private sector and lack of perceived market incentives – which also explains lower incidence of state capture – and the maintenance of a stronger state administration. Uzbekistan's combination of more advanced marketization with widespread controls is a more favorable environment for administrative corruption, as well as some forms of state capture. But in both cases, the continued existence of authoritarian controls may tend to constrain the measurable components of state capture and administrative corruption. As a result, the empirical results would not be comparable with countries that are more advanced in transition.

---

*These same three countries received the lowest scores in the region for political process, civil society, independent media, and democracy, from Freedom House. Karatnycky, Motyl, and Graybow (1998, p16).

Finally, in contrast to administrative corruption, the degree to which a state is captured is not necessarily related to the number of firms that engage in such forms of influence or the amount they spend in doing so. Given that state capture is a function of the concentration of economic power, only a small share of firms can be expected to have the capacity to capture the state. In an extreme case, a single powerful monopoly could generate a much higher level of state capture than a larger number of less powerful firms competing for influence. A measure of state capture, therefore, should be based on the extent to which the state's decisionmaking is distorted by the illicit influence of powerful firms and not necessarily on the number of firms actively exerting such influence.

Despite these caveats, the BEEPS data provide the first opportunity to measure key components of state capture across countries. The survey identified a number of specific activities that fall within the definition of state capture, including: the "sale" of parliamentary votes and presidential decrees to private interests; the sale of civil and criminal court decisions to private interests; corrupt mishandling of central bank funds; and illegal contributions by private actors to political parties.[16] Firms were asked to assess the *direct impact* on their business, either positive or negative, from each of these activities, regardless of whether they engaged in such activities themselves. Thus, capture is measured not by how many firms engage in it, but by the share of firms whose business is directly affected by it.

Table 1.1 presents measures of the share of firms in each country that report a *significant impact* on their business from each one of the indicators of state capture. Clearly, state capture is a significant problem throughout the region across a range of state institutions. Yet the variation across the transition economies is striking. Across the different types of state capture, the sale of parliamentary votes and mishandling of central bank funds are seen as having the most significant and direct impact on firms. Box 1.5 provides a discussion of corruption in the judiciary.

By taking the average of different components of state capture in each country listed in Table 1.1, a general index of state capture can be developed. Though the index aggregates several different forms of state capture affecting different state institutions, it is a useful measure of the perceived extent of the problem across the institutions of the state. It should be recognized, nevertheless, that in developing strategies to combat state capture, it may be necessary to further unbundle the concept itself to identify which institutions within the state are most affected and how the nature of capture differs across these institutions. Figure 1.3 compares this index across the transition countries.

Table 1.1 Share of Firms Affected by Different Forms of State Capture

Country	Parliamentary Legislation	Presidential Decrees	Central Bank	Criminal Courts	Commercial Courts	Political Party Finance	State Capture Index
Albania	12	7	8	22	20	25	16
Armenia	10	7	14	5	6	1	7
Azerbaijan	41	48	39	44	40	35	41
Bulgaria	28	26	28	28	19	42	28
Croatia	18	24	30	29	29	30	27
Czech Rep.	18	11	12	9	9	6	11
Estonia	14	7	8	8	8	17	10
Georgia	29	24	32	18	20	21	24
Hungary	12	7	8	5	5	4	7
Kazakhstan	13	10	19	14	14	6	12
Kyrgyz Rep.	18	16	59	26	30	27	29
Latvia	40	49	8	21	26	35	30
Lithuania	15	7	9	11	14	13	11
Moldova	43	30	40	33	34	42	37
Poland	13	10	6	12	18	10	12
Romania	22	20	26	14	17	27	21
Russia	35	32	47	24	27	24	32
Slovak Rep.	20	12	37	29	25	20	24
Slovenia	8	5	4	6	6	11	7
Ukraine	44	37	37	21	26	29	32
Overall	**24**	**21**	**25**	**18**	**20**	**20**	**21**

Source: Hellman, Jones and Kaufmann (2000a). See the Annex 1 for details.

Figure 1.3. State Capture Index *(share of firms affected by state capture)*

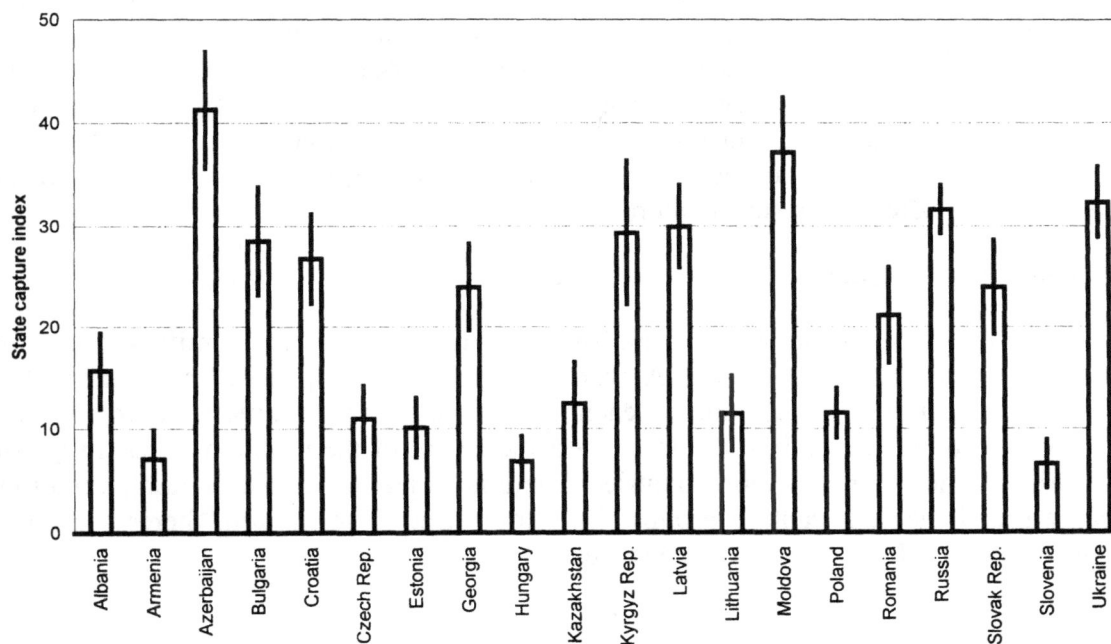

The thin line at the top of each bar represents the statistical margin of error (based on a single standard deviation) calculated for each country within the sample. Source: Hellman, Jones, and Kaufmann (2000a).

14

> **Box 1.5: Corruption in the Judiciary**
>
> Corruption in any institution impedes its operation and distorts its objectives. However, corruption in the judiciary is particularly damaging for several reasons. The legal system is one of the fundamental pillars of a market economy whose role as arbiter of the law encompasses both the formulation and implementation of public policy. In addition to deciding criminal cases, the courts are responsible for upholding property rights, enforcing contracts, and settling disputes. As a result, corruption in the judiciary can display aspects of both state capture and administrative corruption as the terms are used in this report.
>
> Failure of any of these roles is costly, reducing incentives to invest or forcing firms to resort to more costly private means of contract enforcement and protection. In addition to these direct economic costs, a corrupt legal system has a wider impact, undermining the credibility of the state and making the implementation of public policy more difficult. In particular, since the legal system will be the ultimate arbiter of any anticorruption program, a corrupt judiciary will fundamentally undermine anticorruption efforts themselves.

The index shows a rather wide gap between those countries with a high level of state capture and those with a lower level. Beyond a certain threshold level, it would appear that state capture generates a self-reinforcing dynamic pushing toward ever higher levels. According to the index, the following states could be characterized as "high-capture"—Azerbaijan, Bulgaria, Croatia, Georgia, Kyrgyz Republic, Latvia, Moldova, Romania, Russia, Slovak Republic, and Ukraine.

Unlike the measure of administrative corruption, the index of state capture presented above is not based on the behavior of firms, but on the perceptions of firms that such activity affects their business. The BEEPS survey also includes a more direct measure of state capture identifying which firms make unofficial payments to public officials to influence the formation of laws, regulations, or decrees. Only a small share of firms report actively engaging in state capture, ranging from a low of just under 5 percent of firms in Hungary to nearly 15 percent in Latvia. Across all the transition countries, there is a reasonably high correlation (R=0.69) between the number of firms that are actively engaged in capturing the state and the share of firms whose business is affected by state capture.[17]

Developing a Typology of Corruption in Transition

With measures of state capture and administrative corruption, we can identify variation in the *pattern* of corruption across countries. A typology can be developed on the basis of the interaction of both measures of corruption. For each index, countries can be plotted along an axis ranging from "high" to "medium" in order to suggest the extent of the problem of each type of corruption relative to the other transition countries. There is a clear threshold dividing countries into high capture and medium capture groups. On administrative corruption, there is a more continuous distribution of levels across the countries.

Figure 1.4 plots the transition countries according to the indices of administrative corruption and state capture.[18] The scatterplot reveals a considerable degree of dispersion across both indices generating a two-by-two matrix that groups countries by similarities in both the level and pattern of these different dimensions of corruption. Though some countries clearly lie within a particular sphere of the matrix, others have a more ambiguous position, potentially straddling different spheres.

Figure 1.4. Typology of Corruption

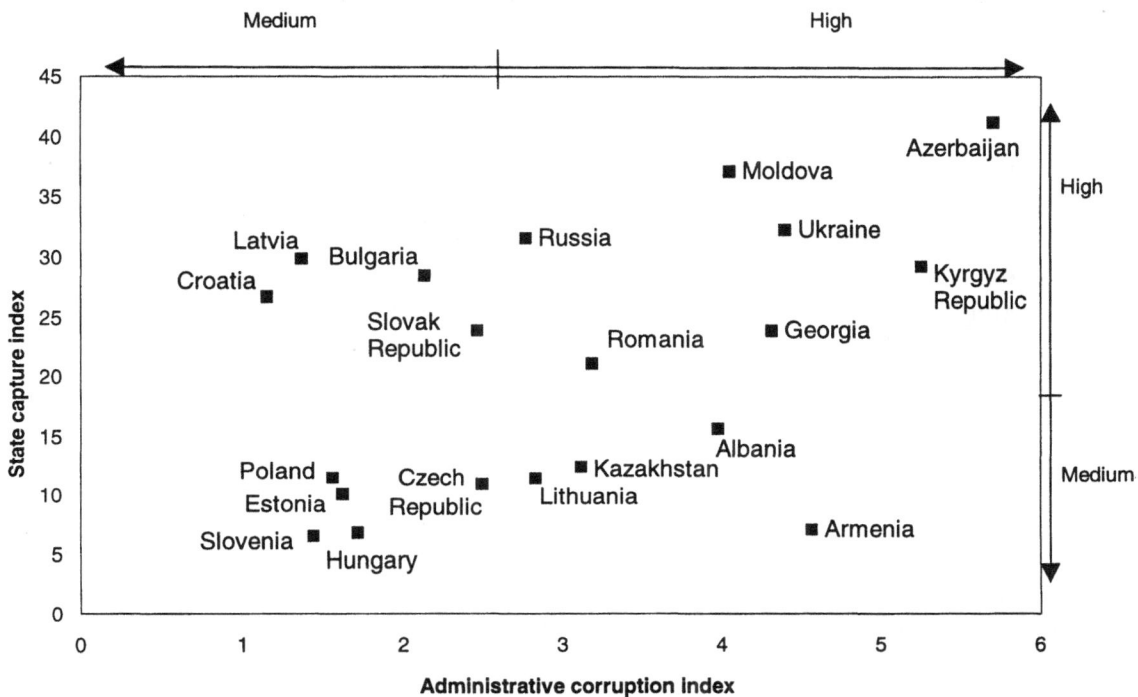

The typology is not intended to define absolute and unambiguous divisions among countries. Rather, it is presented as a heuristic device to highlight analytically and empirically the differences in patterns of corruption across countries. Like all aggregate indices, the measures of administrative corruption and state capture mask important variation across institutions within the state and across actors engaged in these activities. As a result, the typology cannot replace the critical role that individual country studies should play in identifying the extent and nature of the corruption problem and in further unbundling of the forms of corruption identified in the report. Indeed, the typology should be seen more as a guide for self-assessment by countries as to the nature of the corruption problems they face than a definitive categorization of countries on these complex dimensions of corruption.

The typology suggests a classification of four different patterns of corruption:

- In the **high-high** category, a serious problem of administrative corruption—and hence, weak state capacity—is nested in a state highly subject to capture.

- In the **high-medium** category are countries that have been able to contain the level of administrative corruption relative to other transition countries, but nevertheless have done so in a context of high state capture.

- The **medium-high** category includes countries where the problem of administrative corruption remains the central problem, while the state has been less subject to capture by the private sector than have other transition countries.

- Countries in the **medium-medium** category have lower levels of both state capture and administrative corruption than other transition countries, though serious challenges remain.

The typology is a static snapshot taken at the time of the BEEPS survey (mid-1999) of countries engaged in a dynamic process of evolution in both the development of state capture and administrative corruption. How countries evolve into different patterns of corruption and how they might progress (or regress) into different spheres of the typology will be examined in subsequent chapters of this report. Recognizing these different patterns and analyzing alternative evolutionary paths across these patterns could provide a stronger foundation for devising more appropriate and finely tuned anticorruption strategies in different contexts.

---

[1] For the most widely known exposition of this approach, see Klitgaard (1988).

[2] For an early and interesting effort to unbundle analytically the concept of corruption, see Scott (1972). The approach to defining and measuring different dimensions of corruption across countries derives from the following background papers: Hellman, Jones, Kaufmann, and Schankermann (2000); Hellman, Jones, and Kaufmann (2000a).

[3] As a result, the distinction between state capture and administrative corruption does not map directly into the more familiar distinction between "grand corruption" and "petty corruption," which generally refers to the level of state officials engaged in the corrupt transactions. Administrative corruption is most likely to cut across different levels of government, as special discretionary exemptions in the implementation of laws and public procurement decisions are a feature of both the higher and lower levels of government. State capture, by definition, only encompasses levels of government empowered to make legislation, laws, rules, and decrees, though in some systems this could also extend to different levels of government.

[4] For an excellent review of the extensive literature on regulatory capture, see Laffont and Tirole (1993). For a broader discussion of the roots of the concept of state capture, see EBRD *Transition Report 1999*, and Hellman, Jones, and Kaufmann (2000a).

[5] Indeed, the literature on regulatory capture tends to focus much less on corruption than on the inherent information asymmetries in the nature of the relationship between the regulator and the regulated.

[6] The area of public finance corruption is an especially important dimension that could warrant a separate categorization of corruption. Politicians and public officials can alter the mobilization and allocation of public resources and assets for their own private gain. Though this misappropriation of public resources could be classified as a form of administrative corruption, it could be seen to have its own dynamics, especially when such corruption is concentrated at the highest levels of the political system. This would cover instances of kleptocratic political regimes, whose dynamics could be analyzed separately, though many of the normative implications of combating state capture and administrative corruption would still be still relevant to this problem.

[7] For a comprehensive description of the methodology and contents of the survey, as well as a descriptive analysis of the key findings, see Hellman, Jones, Kaufmann, and Schankerman (2000a).

[8] The most frequently used index of corruption is Transparency International's Corruption Perceptions Index, which is a survey of surveys based on outside assessments of corruption and on a particular methodology subject to changes over time (as well as its country coverage, which even though it has grown over the years, currently covers only about one-half of all countries for which there is data). Any such aggregate comparative index will have serious limitations in diagnosing in-depth governance and corruption challenges within a country. For that purpose, a new set of diagnostic survey tools (for public officials, enterprises, and citizens) has been developed under a separate project to help countries in addressing governance challenges, see Kaufmann, Pradhan, and Ryterman (1998).

[9] For an analysis of existing governance and corruption indicators, see Kaufmann, Kraay, and Zoido-Lobaton (1999a and b).

[10] See Annex 1 for a description of the summary indicator.

[11] It is possible that the manifestations of corrupt transactions across countries vary systematically with the level of economic or political development, shifting from explicit bribe payments to more subtle types of benefits such as equity stakes or commitments to future employment. If so, then measurements of corruption that rely exclusively on explicit payments might understate the level of corruption in more developed countries.

[12] See Annex 1.

[13] The rankings of countries on this index of administrative corruption do not change significantly when statistically controlling for the size and sector of firms.

[14] For more detailed information on these household surveys, see Box 5.8: Diagnosing the Problem.

[15] Other transition countries that might be considered in a similar category, including Tajikistan and Turkmenistan, were not included in the BEEPS survey sample.

[16] The decision to include the sale of court decisions to private interests and the mishandling of central bank funds as elements of state capture requires some explanation. Courts are generally seen as institutions that implement existing laws as opposed to making them, though the precedent-setting function of courts can blur these boundaries. In the transition countries, where legal systems are still in the nascent stages of development, courts can be seen as playing a more formative role in the development of the legal framework. As regards the central bank, the institution's role in setting monetary policy and creating the regulatory framework for the developing financial system also blurs the distinction between the formation and implementation of rules. While recognizing the difficulty of drawing concrete boundaries within any particular institution, we have chosen to incorporate these institutions within the category of state capture as a result of the unique nature of the transition period. Yet it is important to note that removing these components from the index of state capture does not change substantially the ranking of countries on state capture presented in Figure 1.3. Moreover, this does not have any effect on the positions of countries in the typology presented in Figure 1.4, which guides much of the empirical work in subsequent chapters. See Annex 1.

[17] By identifying "captor" firms, we can investigate the direct benefits and costs to such firms from engaging in capture. A summary of these results is presented in Chapter Two.

[18] Only countries included in the BEEPS survey are plotted in the typology, which thus excludes: Bosnia and Herzegovina, FYR Macedonia, Tajikistan and Turkmenistan. Though Belarus and Uzbekistan were included in the BEEPS survey, their results are discussed separately in Box 1.4 in recognition of the very different dynamics of state capture in countries that have made minimal progress in transition.

Chapter 2: The Economic and Social Consequences of Corruption in Transition Countries

In recent years, many studies have presented powerful empirical evidence on the economic and social costs of corruption.[1] They have shown how corruption hinders investment (both domestic and foreign), reduces growth, restricts trade, distorts the size and composition of government expenditure, weakens the financial system, and strengthens the underground economy. Most importantly, a strong connection has been demonstrated between corruption and increasing levels of poverty and income inequality. The experience of the transition countries strongly supports these findings. Yet unbundling corruption in transition reveals the extent to which these costs vary as a result of different patterns of corruption.

The costs of state capture and administrative corruption are mutually reinforcing and are themselves influenced by a range of other factors. The fiscal distortions caused by corruption, for example, erode the quality of government services, with particularly serious consequences for the poor. The negative effects of corruption on investment and growth similarly exacerbate poverty and erode the tax base, further undermining the quality of public services. Though this chapter will examine the consequences of corruption in a range of independent areas— growth and investment, poverty and inequality, fiscal stability, public service provision, and government credibility—the mutually reinforcing nature of these costs and the complex lines of causation should always be kept in mind.

Investment and Growth

It is well established that investment is significantly affected by the level of uncertainty in the business environment. By increasing uncertainty, corruption raises the effective cost of investment for the firm and

---

Typology Charts

For the purposes of analysis in the following chapters, the countries have been divided into four groups on the basis of thresholds of administrative corruption and state capture as in Figure 1.4. This produces a two-by-two matrix that groups countries on the basis of similarities in both the level and pattern of corruption. However, it is important to recognize that the composition of the groups is based on the determination of the dividing lines, which is done here for analytical purposes only. As several countries lay close to the thresholds, their inclusion into either group is subject to a greater margin of error. For a graphical depiction of the matrix along with the margins of error, see Annex 1.

Charts such as the one below will be used throughout this report. These charts show the averages of the relevant variable for the countries in each group of the two-by-two matrix. The charts illustrate *associations* between the relevant variable, administrative corruption and state capture, rather than causation. These associations do not take into account the potential explanatory significance of other variables that might influence the associations.

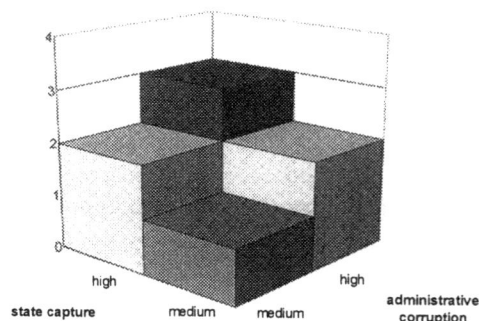

countries having high levels of both administrative corruption and state capture, gross domestic investment averages more than 20 percent less than in countries in the medium/medium category of our typology.[3]

The negative effects of corruption are particularly clear from the firm-level performance data. The average annual sales growth over the past three years was 17 percent for firms reporting moderate levels of administrative corruption, declining to 10 percent for firms reporting higher levels. The differential for investment growth is equally stark: 17 percent versus 9 percent, respectively. The differences hold regardless of firm size, origins, and line of business. It is difficult to establish the direction of causality in this relationship. Weak firms might be more inclined to rely on administrative corruption as a survival mechanism. Alternatively, administrative corruption could directly weaken firm performance, raising questions as to whether such bribery yields any selective benefits for the firm.

The effects of state capture on firm performance show a marked contrast. Where state capture is reported to be prevalent, firms that pay bribes to influence the content of laws, decrees, and regulations show significant *increases* in sales growth.[4] In such environments, firms engaging in capture grew by over 30 percent in the past three years, compared to a growth rate of only 8 percent among other firms. Yet in countries where state capture is limited, engaging in capture does not appear to bring any specific gains to the firm in terms of sales growth. Though capture would appear to create an uneven playing field in certain contexts concentrating gains to powerful firms, high levels of state capture are nevertheless associated with lower firm growth rates overall—sales growth in low-capture countries averages 21 percent, compared to only 11 percent in high capture countries. The gains to capture for particular firms appear to be associated with negative consequences for less influential firms.[5] Again, the issue of the direction of causality could be raised—capture could directly improve firm performance or stronger firms could be more likely to engage in capture.[6]

Though a small group of firms appears to receive gains from capture in certain contexts, the social costs of capture are substantial. State capture represents a transfer of wealth among politicians, firms, and the state via distortions in the underlying competitive and institutional framework. Figure 2.1 shows that countries with high levels of state capture and administrative corruption had the largest output decline in the period 1989-98.[7] Though the direction of causation is ambiguous, a strong case can be made that corruption contributed to the output decline, given its effects on investment and growth, the weakening of tax revenues, the misappropriation of credits and subsidies, and the erosion of public sector services.

Figure 2.1. Corruption and Output Decline

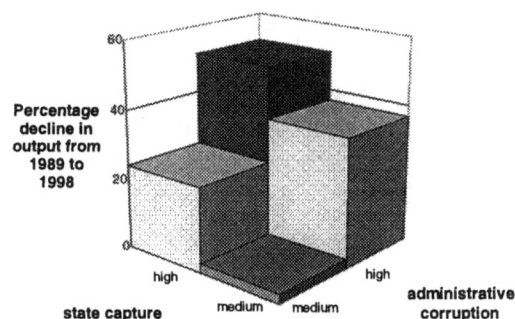

Data Source: BEEPS and EBRD

Poverty[8]

For so many individuals and families, the most immediate and visible consequence of the transition has been a decline in their living standards. Even among the more advanced reformers, poverty levels have expanded over the past decade at an alarming rate, as demonstrated in the Prague 2000 report *Making the Transition Work for Everyone*. The expansion of poverty was initiated by the collapse of GDP, which fell by 50 percent in the CIS countries and 15 percent in CEE. Yet even with recovery, poverty rates have remained high as incomes of the poor have failed to recover and inadequate social safety nets have left the most vulnerable groups unprotected.

Figure 2.2 demonstrates that poverty is highly correlated with administrative corruption.[9] Surely, poverty can contribute to corruption as poor countries have fewer resources to implement and maintain the monitoring and oversight necessary to contain the problem.[10] Yet corruption also exacerbates poverty. As demonstrated above, corruption is empirically associated with lower economic growth rates, weakening the main factor that can pull people out of poverty. Moreover, corruption has a direct impact on the living conditions of the poor.[11]

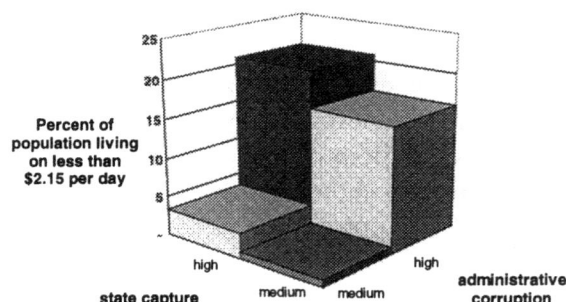

Figure 2.2. Corruption and Poverty

Percent of population living on less than $2.15 per day

state capture — administrative corruption

Data Source: BEEPS and World Bank

Corruption and service delivery: When corruption misdirects the assignment of unemployment or disability benefits, delays eligibility for pensions, weakens the provision of basic public services, it is usually the poor who suffer most. Such corruption undermines the social safety net and may deter the poor from seeking basic entitlements and other public services.

Bribery at the household level: The extent to which households engage in bribery is strongly correlated with both administrative corruption and state capture as demonstrated by a UNICRI cross-country survey of more than 25,000 households in 20 transition countries.[12] For example, in a country like Georgia, with high levels of both state capture and administrative corruption, nearly 30 percent of households said they paid a bribe in the previous year, in marked contrast to Slovenia where only 1.5 percent of households reported bribe payments. Though corruption at the household level affects people at all income levels, the poor again appear to be most seriously affected. Detailed household surveys show that the poor are the least likely to know how to get proper treatment when an official abuses his position. In Latvia, for example, only 31 percent of households in the poorest third of the population knew how to seek recourse to deal with corrupt service provision, compared to 42 percent among the richest third of the population.[13]

Effect on small and micro enterprises: Within the economy, corruption is a highly regressive tax as the BEEPS data demonstrate. Small enterprises across the region pay, on average, more than twice as much of their annual revenue in bribes as do large firms. Such firms are particularly hard hit by administrative corruption. Microentrepreneurs appear to be prime targets for corruption. Household surveys in several transition countries demonstrate that bribery at the household level is most strongly associated with participation in a microenterprise. In Georgia, for example, poor households that earn unofficial income were four times more likely to pay bribes than households without unofficial income. Corruption clearly hinders the ability of the poor to help themselves out of poverty.

Inequality

As examined in the Prague 2000 report *Making the Transition Work for Everyone*, inequality within the transition countries has increased at an alarming pace. In some countries of the region inequality has now reached levels on par with the most unequal Latin American countries. Though numerous factors contribute to the growth in inequality, corruption should also be seen as a contributing factor. As the data on firm performance demonstrated, state capture concentrates substantial gains to a narrow group of firms in a position to encode their advantages in the basic legislative, legal, and regulatory frameworks that govern the economy. By capturing the state, the "early winners" of transition gained fabulous wealth taking advantage of arbitrage opportunities associated with partial reforms and laying claim to state assets at highly undervalued prices. Privatization, in particular, became a key focus for state capture in some transition countries as some firms and political structures used illegitimate forms of influence to concentrate productive assets in their hands.[14] In contrast, the poor gained little, if at all, from the redistribution of what were once "social" assets. While the interaction between corruption and income inequality is certainly complex, the ultimate result has been clear: income inequality has expanded most in countries with high levels of corruption and capture, as demonstrated in Figure 2.3.[15]

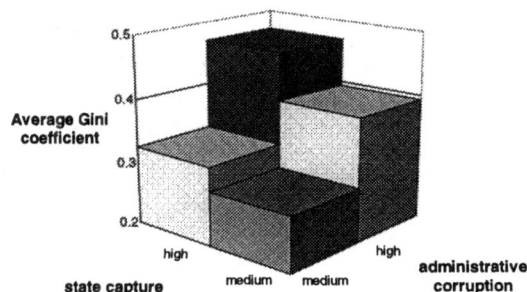

Figure 2.3. Corruption and Income Inequality

Average Gini coefficient

Data Source: BEEPS and World Bank

Fiscal Implications

While increasing private revenues to public officials, corruption tends to have a negative impact on public revenues. This impact operates through a number of channels. First, as the surveys demonstrate, a substantial share of administrative corruption is directed towards tax and customs officials, presumably resulting in lower tax and customs payments by firms.[16] In the BEEPS survey, one in nine firms said they frequently make unofficial payments to tax inspectors or customs officials, while half of the firms did so at least occasionally.[17] Such corruption represents a substantial indirect private transfer in many countries from the budget to public officials.

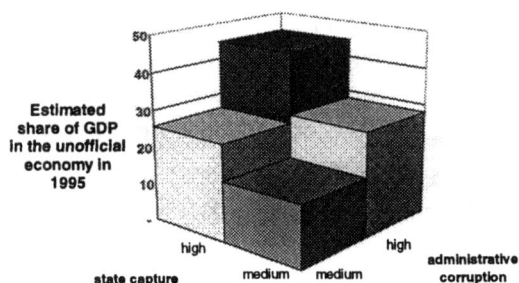

Figure 2.4. The Unofficial Economy

Estimated share of GDP in the unofficial economy in 1995

Data Source: BEEPS and Johnson, Kaufmann, and Shleifer (1997)

Second, as is clear in Figure 2.4,[18] corruption is closely associated with the unofficial economy, the

22

size of which can have profound fiscal implications in many transition countries.[19] When firms produce for the unofficial economy, they underreport economic activity or avoid the state entirely. This creates competitive advantages that can drive honest competitors from the market, thereby generating further corruption and fiscal shrinkage.[20] The reduction of tax revenues reduces the funds available for public services, providing firms with fewer incentives to operate officially. Once underground, such firms pay bribes to avoid detection and punishment. The fiscal implications in some countries have been staggering. In Ukraine, the government recently offered an amnesty for an estimated US$20 billion in "gray capital" kept offshore.[21]

Third, corruption in procurement, assignment of subsidies, and outright theft leads to an exaggerated flow of funds out of the public coffers. Corruption in procurement, for example, leads to waste of public resources for often inferior quality products and services, and ultimately may deter honest vendors from doing business with the state. In a survey in Georgia, the need to make unofficial payments was the most cited reason that firms said they do not participate in state tenders.[22]

The fiscal weaknesses exacerbated by administrative corruption and state capture contribute to weak macroeconomic performance. As Figure 2.5 shows, transition countries with the lowest levels of administrative corruption and state capture have the most effective institutions for macroeconomic governance.[23] Though macroeconomic instability certainly creates a fertile ground for corruption, the fiscal implications described above suggest that corruption contributes to the macroeconomic instability as well.

Figure 2.5. Quality of Macroeconomic Governance

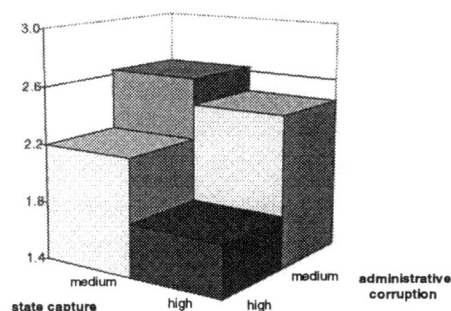

Data Source: BEEPS

Credibility of the State

As later chapters of the report will demonstrate, combating corruption requires strong and credible political leadership. Yet this is precisely the aspect of the political system that is most seriously undermined by administrative corruption and state capture.[24] The BEEPS data confirm that approval ratings for the key institutions of government drop sharply with increasing levels of state capture and administrative corruption: only 38 percent of firms in countries in the high-high category of the typology expressed satisfaction with the political leadership, compared to 56 percent in the other transition countries. Firms in the high-high category also expressed the least confidence in the capacity of the legal system to uphold their property and contract rights: 58 percent of firms in these countries complained of insecure property and contract rights, compared to 35 percent of firms in the medium-medium category. Corruption erodes trust in the institutions of state, which in turn weakens the state's capacity to fight corruption. A 1999 household survey in the Slovak Republic confirms the point: respondents who believed that corruption was widespread were more than twice as likely to doubt the credibility of the government's anticorruption campaign than those who perceived corruption to be more limited.[25]

A dangerous byproduct of this erosion of trust is increasing crime. Problems with both organized crime and street crime are highly correlated with state capture and administrative corruption. As Figure 2.6 suggests, more than twice as many firms in countries in the high-high category identify organized crime as an obstacle to their business than in the medium-medium group of countries.

Figure 2.6. Organized Crime as a Problem Doing Business

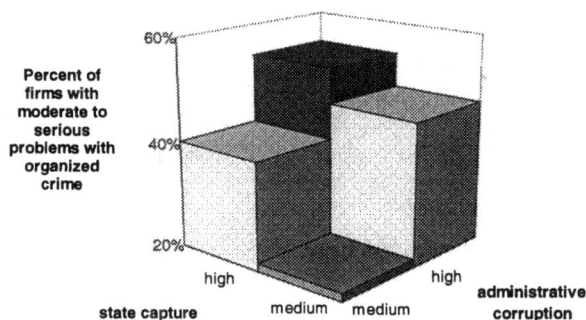

Data Source: BEEPS

Ultimately, corruption, capture and distrust feed on each other, deepening and entrenching the problems. If and when political leaders committed to fighting corruption arrive on the scene, in many countries they face a cynical population that has strong doubts about the credibility of the state. Where states have been captured, reformers must overcome a deep chasm of distrust before an anticorruption program can take hold. Yet by failing to address the problem of corruption, they are confronted by a vicious circle of lower investment and growth, higher poverty and inequality, greater fiscal imbalances, and weaker delivery of basic public services.

---

[1] Studies include: Mauro (1995, 1997, 1998), Wei (1999a, 1999b, 2000), Campos, Lien, and Pradhan (1999), Kaufmann (1997), Tanzi (1998), Tanzi and Davoodi (1997), Kaufmann and Wei (1999), Wei and Sievers (1999), Johnson, Kaufmann, and Zoido-Lobaton (1998a), Johnson, Kaufmann, and Shleifer (1997), Gupta, Davoodi, and Alonso-Terme (1998), Anderson and Marcouiller (1999).

[2] Corruption is also a notorious deterrent of foreign direct investment. However, since foreign investment is often motivated by abundance of natural resources, which is in turn associated with high levels of corruption, the statistical relationship between foreign direct investment, capture, and corruption in transition countries is ambiguous.

[3] Gross domestic investment in 1997 was 27 percent of GDP in countries with medium levels of administrative corruption and state capture, compared to 21 percent in countries with high levels. The difference is significant at the 5 percent level in a pair-wise t-test.

[4] In the BEEPS survey firms were asked how often they make unofficial payments to influence the content of laws, decrees, or regulations. Responses to this question were used to identify "captor" firms, whose individual performance can then be measured. Only a small share of firms (generally less than 5 per cent of the sample in each country) reported engaging in capture. There is, however, a correlation between the number of firms that report engaging in state capture and the number of firms that report experiencing a significant impact on their business from state capture. See Hellman, Jones, and Kaufmann (2000a).

[5] This remains true even after accounting for other factors, such as firm size, sector, ownership, and origin, that influence firm performance.

[6] Though it would be difficult to assert the direction of causality with certainty, there are indications that the gains to firms come as a result of capture. First, bribing to influence rules and laws is more likely to be a voluntary transaction between the firm and state officials and, hence, unlikely to be a form of direct extortion by state officials. Thus, presumably, firms would not engage in it unless it brought clear advantages. Second, the gains to capture are strongly influenced by the nature of the broader environment in which capture takes place. Capture is associated with specific gains to captor firms only where some threshold of capture has been reached in the country. This strengthens the view that capture actually generates such gains.

[7] See Annex 1.

[8] This section draws on Anderson and others (1999). See also Gupta, Davoodi, and Alonso-Term (1998), Dethier (1999a, 1999b).

[9] See Annex 1.

[10] Treisman (2000) found evidence that economic development may lead to lower corruption.

[11] Recent empirical studies on corruption's disproportionate impact on the poor include Knack and Anderson (1999) and Gupta, Davoodi, and Alonso-Terme (1998). See also Narayan and others (2000) for the impact of corruption on the poor in the words of the poor themselves.

[12] The International Crime Victim Survey was carried out in transition countries in 1996 and 1997. Country-level statistics are reported in Zvekic (1998).

[13] Anderson, Dethier, Dudwick, Kuehnast, and Shkaratan (1999).

[14] EBRD (1999) finds that for a given level of privatization the quality of governance in countries with relatively low levels of capture is substantially higher than in countries with higher levels of state capture.

[15] See Annex 1.

[16] However, administrative corruption payments in the areas of tax and customs administration are often paid to reduce the discretionary power of bureaucrats to levy taxes and customs rather than to reduce standardized tax and customs levels.

[17] In virtually every country where detailed surveys have been undertaken, the customs service is identified as an organization in which bribes are frequently paid. Examples include Albania (Kaufmann, Pasha, Preci, Ryterman, and Zoido-Lobaton (1998)), Georgia (Anderson, Azfar, Kaufmann, Lee, Mukherjee, and Ryterman (1999), Tajikistan (Mirzoev (1999)), Ukraine (survey by "Intellectual Business Foundation," cited in Holovaty (2000)). Even in more developed transition countries, customs is noted by enterprises as one of the organizations at which bribery is common: Latvia (Anderson (1998)), and the Slovak Republic (Anderson (2000)).

[18] See Annex 1.

[19] Johnson, Kaufmann, and Shleifer (1997), Johnson, Kaufmann, and Zoido-Lobaton (1998a, 1998b), Schneider and Enste (1998).

[20] This vicious circle has been explored by Johnson, Kaufmann, and Shleifer (1997) and by Johnson, Kaufmann, and Zoido-Lobaton (1998a and b). "The unofficial economy accounts for a larger share of GDP when there is higher bureaucratic inefficiency and discretion, and also when firms experience a higher tax and regulatory burden and more bribery and corruption."

[21] *Financial Times*, April 3, 2000.

[22] Anderson, Azfar, Kaufmann, Lee, Mukherjee, and Ryterman (1999).

[23] Macroeconomic governance is an index measuring the extent to which policy instability, exchange rate instability, and inflation are an obstacle to business. See EBRD (1999) "Transition Report 1999: Chapter 6 - Governance in Transition" and Annex 1 for details.

[24] The findings described here are consistent with recent empirical work showing that levels of trust are higher in countries with lower levels of bribery. Zak and Knack (1998).

[25] Anderson (2000).

Chapter 3: The Origins of Corruption in Transition Countries

The transition from socialism is a unique historical process. Never before have countries attempted such a radical and simultaneous transformation of both their political and economic institutions. Underpinning these transformations has been a complex set of reforms that entail building the basic institutions of state, creating the foundations of a market economy and transferring wealth from the state to the private sector on a large scale.

Why has the transition been marked by state capture and administrative corruption? Certainly, corruption has deep roots and existed in these countries long before transition. Due to fundamental differences in the nature of corruption in market and nonmarket economies, it is difficult to compare the levels of corruption before transition with the current period. Hence, it is impossible to provide definitive evidence of the effect of transition on corruption. But it is clear that the simultaneity of political and economic reform that characterizes the process of transition has introduced scope in some nations for powerful interests to influence the structure of state institutions and the formulation and implementation of economic policy to their own advantage.[1] Corruption in this setting has been facilitated by three factors: (i) the rewriting of an unprecedented volume of laws, regulations, and policies; (ii) the extraordinary redistribution of wealth from the state to the private sector; and (iii) the virtual absence of institutions either within or external to the public sector that could effectively check the abuse of public office during the transition in many countries.

At the same time, this report demonstrates the considerable variation in levels of state capture and administrative corruption across the region. What factors explain this variation? Part of the answer is rooted in the different institutional and structural legacies with which countries entered the transition. Institutions for public administration were more developed at the onset of transition in certain countries, especially those with a longer experience of sovereignty. Countries with legal and institutional traditions that emphasized the rule of law appear to have begun the transition with an advantage. Previous exposure to market-oriented institutions in those countries that had adopted variants of market socialism may have shaped the receptiveness to reform. Economies with a high level of natural resources are more likely to generate powerful interests seeking to capture states and lay claim to the concentrated gains stemming from such resources.

Institutional legacies and other initial conditions have a strong influence on the "first moves" of the transition process, such as choices about the structure of political institutions and the pace and comprehensiveness of economic reform. These choices set in motion unique transition paths that favor particular economic and social groups and shape incentives for further reforms. Countries where the transition path led to a concentration of economic power in a setting of weak basic institutions became especially vulnerable to state capture and administrative corruption.

While initial conditions explain an important part of the variation in the pattern of corruption in the region, initial conditions tell only part of the story – much of the variation remains unexplained. This feature suggests that other factors, such as the rise of effective leaders who are able to implement and sustain policies that are inimical to corruption, are also critical to the development of the transition path. Through an understanding of the role of initial conditions and especially institutional legacies is crucial for developing effective strategies to combat corruption, this does not imply that some countries were predestined to generate high levels of corruption in the transition. Political will and policy choice have a key role to play in determining the susceptibility of a country to corruption.

Institutional Legacies

Research on the origins of corruption worldwide[2] confirms that corruption is rooted in poorly functioning institutions, as well as in policies that undermine free trade and competition. The nature of the institutional legacies at the start of the transition differed substantially across the region despite the apparent monolithic nature of communism. The main features of this variation are explained below.

Accountability and Repression. The old system entailed the fusion of the state and the economy. Authoritarianism obliterated the separation of the legislative, executive, and judicial functions of state. Most civil liberties were suppressed. Social organizations, such as trade unions, professional clubs, and youth organizations, did exist, but were pervaded by the Communist Party. Civil society as a sphere of interaction autonomous from the state was highly attenuated. When independent social movements did emerge, for example Solidarity in Poland and Charter 77 and later Civic Forum in Czechoslovakia, they were perceived by the Communist Party as threats to its system of control.

The Communist Party attempted to control the behavior of public officials using a mixture of incentives and repression. One key incentive derived from the system of appointing individuals to key positions in government and the economy. These appointees, known as the *nomenklatura*, had special privileges and, as a consequence of their positions, unique access to goods and services in short supply. The Communist Party carefully monitored its officials, using a system of mutual oversight and repression. The internal security services enlisted citizen informants, who provided detailed and often incriminating information on their family, friends, and colleagues.

The very process of central planning also served to limit, to some extent, the discretion of bureaucrats. Economic activity was regulated by plan targets. Centralized control was maintained over financial flows through a monobanking system, in which finance closely followed the plan. Cash emissions and cash transfers were strictly controlled. Foreign trade for the entire economy was monopolized in a highly centralized bureaucratic structure. Though the actual practice of central planning did leave a great deal of discretion to bureaucrats at all levels, the system did place certain boundaries on corruption.

At the onset of transition, most of these controlling structures were formally dismantled, although in many countries they have come to play new roles. New institutions of accountability—to be derived from such models as the separation of state functions, participation by the population in oversight of the state, and better systems of public administration—have been slow to emerge in many countries. Into the vacuum, preexisting *nomenklatura* networks and new economic elites have secured positions of dominance in the transition environment creating a new fusion of economic and political power. In many countries, this has created fertile ground for state capture and administrative corruption.

The Culture of State Intervention. One of the key legacies of communism was a "culture of policymaking" in which the state played the dominant role in intermediating economic relations. Bureaucrats were assimilated into an environment in which the state determined suppliers and customers, set prices and wages, provided finance, controlled distribution, and oversaw most aspects of enterprise behavior. Though many of these instruments of intervention have been abolished or curtailed, a number of them still persist. Old habits remain widespread—especially in countries where bureaucratic turnover in the early years of transition was low— as bureaucrats tend to respond *instinctively* to reports of economic dysfunction or crisis by directly intervening in enterprise affairs.[3]

This ingrained tendency toward state intervention, which varies across the region, creates the potential for corruption, especially when regulated entities have little recourse to appeal unfair treatment. Given that the transition is a period when a significant body of new regulations must be formulated, it also exacerbates the risk that corrupt bureaucrats will enshrine possibilities to extract bribes in the new legal regulatory codes.

Variation Across Countries. Institutional legacies have differed far more across the region than the communist façade had ever revealed. Empirical analysis suggests that these

Figure 3.1. Statehood and Corruption

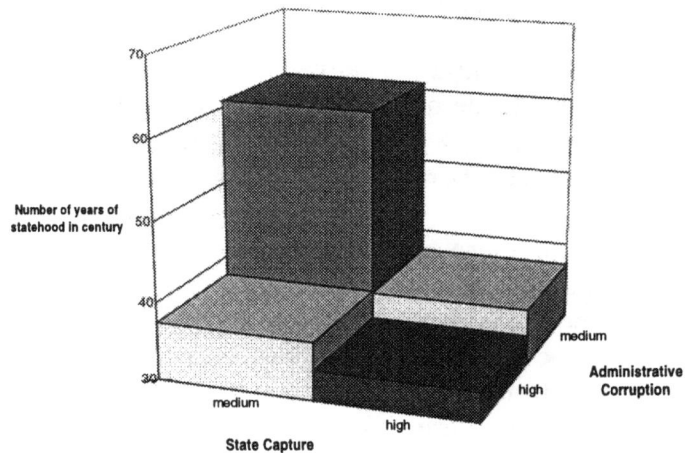

Data Source: BEEPS

differences have had a profound impact on the susceptibility of countries to state capture and administrative corruption through a number of channels.[4] First and foremost, these legacies influenced the level of development of a country's system of public administration. Figure 3.1 shows that countries with a longer experience of sovereignty have faced less dramatic levels of both state capture and administrative corruption.[5] These countries appear to have begun the transition with more developed public-sector institutions and better-trained officials.

As shown in Figure 3.2,[6] countries that were formerly part of the Habsburg Monarchy appear to have benefited from the former empire's legacy of a strong civil service and judicial administration, as well as closer contacts with the West.[7] They were also

Figure 3.2. Habsburg Legacy and Corruption

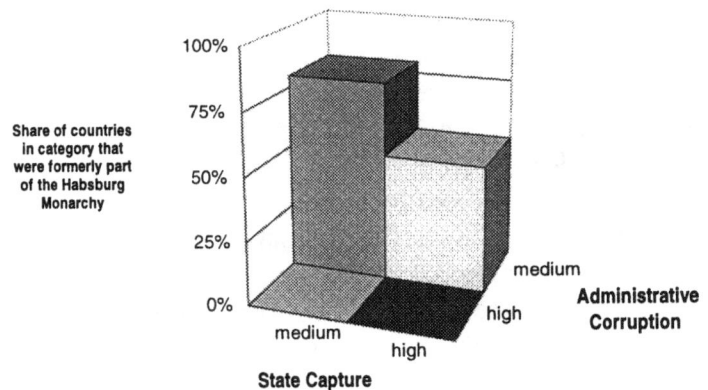

Data Source: BEEPS

more likely to have adopted variants of socialism during the communist period (i.e., market socialism and labor management), which provided for a smaller role of the state in the economy and greater development of market institutions. One important consequence of these mutually reinforcing legacies of stronger public administration and a reduced role of the state is less administrative corruption.

Many of the countries with a longer history of sovereignty also have more developed civil societies and a stronger tradition of collective action as part of their political process. The tendency under communism for social movements to try periodically to assert a liberal political and economic agenda was particularly strong in Central Europe and in other countries where civil society had historically played the largest role. These countries were among the first to realize the delicate relationship between economic growth and democracy, and initiated reforms beginning in the 1960s aimed at political and economic liberalization. While many of these reforms were later suppressed, these experiences provided a blueprint for the way in which social movements could have a profound impact on the process of change. In fact, countries with the strongest traditions of democracy were led into transition by opposition movements and have emerged, not coincidentally, as the states least vulnerable to capture by a concentrated set of private interests,[8] as shown in Figure 3.3.[9]

Figure 3.3. Democracy and Corruption

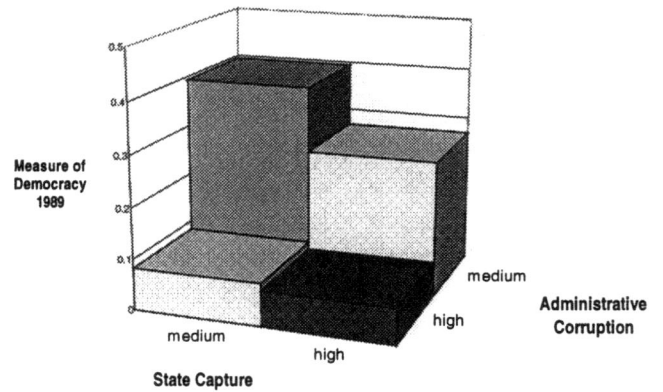

Data Source: BEEPS and Adelman and Vujovic, 1997.

Economic Legacies

Incentives rooted in the structure of the economy also appear to have played a crucial role in explaining the variation in the level and pattern of corruption across the region. In some countries where national wealth is concentrated in a few highly productive assets, potential 'windfall gains' have tempted powerful individuals or economic groups to engage in state capture. Efforts by private interests to lay claim to these assets and then to build anticompetitive barriers to protect their assets have been in evidence in Azerbaijan, Russia, Kazakhstan, and Turkmenistan, all richly endowed with natural resources, as well as in many countries along the transit routes for the distribution and sale of these resources. Figure 3.4 suggests that across the region state capture has been more prevalent in countries well endowed with natural resources.[10]

Figure 3.4. Resource Endowments and Corruption

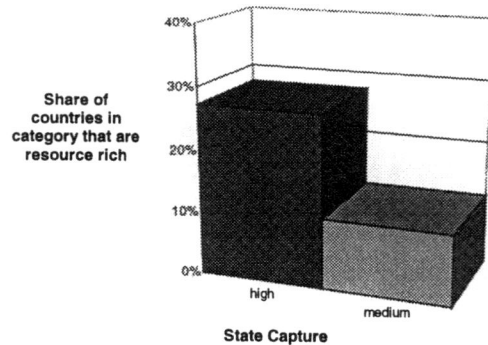

Data Source: BEEPS

In most transition countries, dramatic declines in output and dislocations associated with the transition sharply reduced public revenues. As inflation soared in the early stages of transition, real wages in the public sector fell substantially. In many countries, salaries for bureaucrats at the start of transition had fallen below subsistence levels. Moreover, weak payments discipline and budgetary shortfalls meant that public sector workers were often not paid for months at a time. In such an environment, bureaucrats become vulnerable to corruption as they search for ways to supplement meager wages.[11]

Transition Paths

Variations in these institutional and economic legacies across countries in the region, often referred to as "initial conditions," have already been shown to have had an important effect on the outcomes of transition.[12] These initial conditions influenced the early choices about the basic structure of the political institutions governing the transition as well as the speed and comprehensiveness of the first moves on economic reform. As a result, countries began to follow divergent transition paths from the very beginning, with equally divergent outcomes in terms of economic performance and the extent and pattern of corruption.

In many of the Central and Eastern European countries, the transition was launched and fundamentally shaped in the early stages by broad-based coalitions within civil society. The initial political institutions were forged, in many of these cases, through roundtable negotiations representing a wide range of social groups and political movements. In the CIS, in contrast, the transition was largely initiated from the top down and, in some countries, even came as a *fait accompli* following the disintegration of the Soviet Union. In much of the CIS, the existing Communist Party leadership managed the early stages of transition and civic participation remained weak. The difference between these alternative exit routes from the communist system, which is illustrated in Box 3.1 by a comparison of Poland and Russia, has had powerful implications for the establishment of political accountability within these countries.

Box 3.1. Comparison of the Transition in Poland and Russia

The way in which institutions and incentives can work together to create or obstruct opportunities for corruption is well illustrated by a comparison of two neighboring countries: Poland and Russia. Poland has a long history of sovereignty,[13] having adopted orthodox socialism only after the Second World War. Shortly following Khrushchev's denunciation of Stalin in 1956, a worker's strike in Poznan led to the introduction of market socialism and limited civil liberties. Periodic strikes over the next two decades created episodic pressure to reform, and eventually led in 1980 to the emergence of Solidarity, a trade union which, together with the Catholic Church, became the basis for an effective opposition movement to the Communist Party. In Poland, 10 million people— one in two adults—were members of Solidarity at the start of the transition. In 1989, 29 delegates from the Party, 26 from Solidarity, and 3 Church observers met in three working groups, or roundtables, which culminated in the emergence of a parliamentary political system with proportional representation and an approach toward economic reform that was built upon a social consensus and thus an *encompassing* set of social interests.[14] These choices, in combination with Poland's comparatively stronger skills in public administration, appear to have placed certain limits on the extent to which state capture and administrative corruption could emerge.

Russia and many other countries in the former Soviet Union entered the transition in a completely different way. Unlike in Poland and other Central European countries, political and economic liberalization—*glasnost* and *perestroika*, respectively—were not initiated by civil society, but by the Communist Party leadership. Following the break-up of the Soviet Union and the emergence of new states, choices about the structure of the political system and the initial economic reform program were not made through a process of broad social consultation and consensus, but by an elite group of reformers in a style reflective of Russia's autocratic past. Like many other countries in the CIS, Russia adopted a presidential system with highly concentrated executive powers and weak institutional restraints within the state. Without the benefit of institutional safeguards, the process of economic reform became especially vulnerable to capture by a *narrow* set of private interests eager to garner control over lucrative state assets, especially the highly prized natural resource companies.

Figure 3.5 shows that countries in which there was a clear break with the past leadership at the start of transition have a significantly lower incidence of state capture, as well as administrative corruption.[15] Early change in leadership is one indicator of the extent to which existing networks of power and influence inherited from the old system were broken up and faced with competition from alternative elites.[16] Such change not only brought in new talent often oriented toward reform, but also created new mechanisms of political accountability, in many cases rooted in political competition and enhanced participation by civil society.

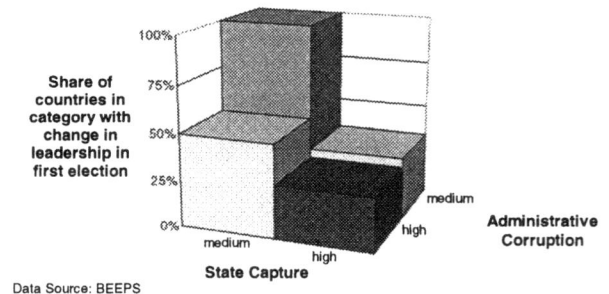
Figure 3.5. Change in Leadership and Corruption
Data Source: BEEPS

One of the most controversial measures taken by some countries to ensure a break with the past is a policy known as *lustration*.[17] This policy, which was adopted in the Czech Republic, Poland, and Estonia, among other countries, prohibits former officials of the internal security apparatus and their informants from accepting public-sector employment. In sharp contrast, officials of the Communist regime and remnants of the internal security apparatus continue to retain important political and economic positions in such countries as Kazakhstan, Uzbekistan, Turkmenistan, Tajikistan, Belarus, Armenia, and Azerbaijan. Although the power structure in

Russia became more diffuse in the 1990s, old patronage networks and clan structures are particularly strong in various regions and republics within Russia.[18]

The nature and extent of the break with the old regime set in motion the main driving forces of alternative transition paths, namely the pace and comprehensiveness of political and economic reforms and personal freedoms. These factors can be considered the key transmission mechanisms creating the conditions for different levels of state capture. Figure 3.6 demonstrates the relationship between economic reforms and civil liberties and the extent of state capture across the region.[19] In fitted regressions, the level of state capture is lowest in the systems with lowest and highest levels of civil liberties.

In the most authoritarian systems in the region, the capacity of independent private firms—to the extent that an independent private sector exists at all—to capture the state is minimal. In such countries, firms generally remain subordinated to the state, both in terms of ownership and control, and have little capacity to influence government decisionmaking. However, though state capture by private firms is low in such systems, other forms of capture—such as capture of the state by political leaders to benefit their own private interests—may be more prevalent, given the lack of accountability on such leaders. Unfortunately, the state capture index used in this report does not measure such forms of the problem.

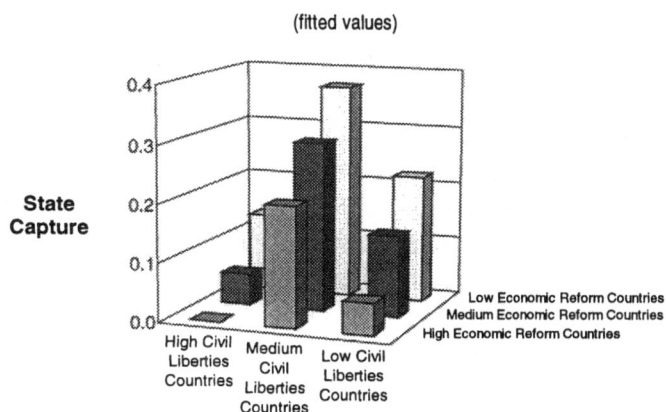

Figure 3.6. Economic Reform, Civil Liberties, and State Capture

(fitted values)

Data Source: BEEPS; Freedom House; Hellman, Jones, and Kaufmann, 2000a.

The environment for state capture by private firms does appear to be generated by a certain minimal threshold of political and economic reforms. Partial political reforms that break with the previous communist system but do not provide new mechanisms of accountability such as political competition, internal checks and balances, or civil society oversight generate the greatest opportunities for a narrow set of private sector interests to capture the state. In these countries, the extent of civil liberties (and other checks on abuse of power) is insufficient to counterbalance the loss of control that resulted from the dismantling of the communist system. Yet the figure suggests that once a threshold of political reforms has been crossed, the extent of state capture inherent in the transition process can be constrained to significantly lower levels.

Figure 3.6 also illustrates the potential interaction between political and economic liberalization in reducing capture. The countries of the region have been grouped into three levels of economic reform—high, medium and low—based on their average scores on EBRD's transition indicators, an annual measure of progress in transition across nine areas of liberalization and structural reform. For any given level of progress on civil liberties, the figure suggests that progress in economic transition is associated with lower levels of capture. Of course, cause and effect are difficult to untangle in these complex and highly interdependent processes. There is much evidence to suggest that the pace and comprehensiveness of economic reforms reduces economic rents associated with distortions in a partially reformed economy. Reducing the concentration of economic rents weakens the incentives for private sector actors to invest the considerable costs, in terms of money, time, and influence, necessary to engage in state capture. At the same time, the processes of deregulation and limitation of the powers of the state to intervene in the economy reduce the range of laws, regulations, and policies that are potentially "for sale."

The progress of both political and economic reforms is in itself partly an outcome of the level of state capture in a given country. Those with the power and resources to capture the state can have a vested interest in preventing reforms that threaten their influence or eliminate the economic distortions on which their concentrated private gains are based.[20] As a result, partial political and economic reforms appear to generate state capture which, in turn, weakens the power and capacity of the state to pursue such reforms further. This accounts for the difficulty of emerging from state capture once it takes hold. But it also suggests that when political will has been marshaled through critical elections, through the entry of new collective actors into the political and civil arena, and through exogenous pressures and opportunities, progress in political and economic reforms has had a powerful impact in reducing state capture.

The Redistribution of Assets

In addition to the simultaneous processes of creating new political and economic institutions, a key characteristic of the transition has been the massive redistribution of assets from social ownership to private ownership. It is perhaps this redistribution, highly concentrated in time, that has provided the strongest incentives for capturing the state in the transition countries. By capturing the state in the process of privatization, private actors sought to transform their *de facto* political influence into *de jure* ownership stakes that would secure their advantages in the emerging market economy. Numerous examples exist in all countries in transition where ownership or control of key state assets was transferred through nontransparent means to those with political influence; corruption has played a key part in this process.

Perhaps the most prominent example of nontransparent privatization in the region has been the loans-for-shares scheme, which was implemented in Russia in the fall of 1995. According to this scheme, the Russian government obtained short-term credit from major Russian banks using its shares in Russian enterprises as collateral. When the government defaulted, the banks were able to keep the shares. The implicit prices on these shares were well below their market value.[21]

Nontransparent privatization has not only been a problem in Russia and the CIS countries. In October 1994, the head of the Czech privatization agency was caught taking a bribe equal to about US$300,000 in connection to the sale of a dairy.[22] In Hungary, eight of the ten members of the privatization agency were forced to resign in October 1994, following allegations of corruption in the sale of formerly state-owned enterprises.

Unfortunately, there is little systematic research on the conditions that make particular methods of privatization more or less vulnerable to corruption.[23] Early in the transition, many observers believed that mass privatization offered governments a simple and transparent mechanism for transferring the bulk of state assets to the general population. Despite the simplicity of the method, enterprise managers were often able to manipulate the market value of their firms or exploit weaknesses in institutional arrangements for shareholder protection in order to be able to retain control. These methods included illegally threatening workers who sold shares to outsiders and issuing new shares in order to dilute the power of outsiders.[24]

Privatization through a case-by-case method, while complex and time-consuming, has allowed some countries to structure the sale of the assets to avoid some of the problems associated with state capture, though this method has also been open to abuse. Large privatizations are vulnerable to corruption whatever the method employed, as the experience of advanced countries frequently demonstrates. Recognizing this temptation, some governments, such as Romania, have delegated responsibility for organizing privatization to internationally recognized investment firms.

The Role of Foreign Investment and Assistance

It is often suggested that inflows of foreign direct investment (FDI) can help reduce corruption by importing higher standards of corporate behavior with potentially powerful demonstration effects in local markets.[25] Others argue, in contrast, that FDI can increase the level of corruption as foreign actors use bribery and other forms of influence to penetrate new markets where they lack existing contacts and networks.

Figure 3.7 depicts the relationship between FDI and corruption using data from the BEEPS survey.[26] Firms are divided into three groups: (i) domestic firms with no FDI; (ii) firms with FDI headquartered in the domestic market; and (iii) firms with FDI headquartered overseas. The charts depict the propensity of each of these firm types across the region to pay bribes for administrative corruption and to engage in state capture through bribery to influence laws, decrees, and regulations. FDI firms headquartered in the local market face similar levels of administrative corruption as domestically owned firms and are just as likely to engage in state capture.[27] However, FDI firms headquartered abroad do report substantially lower levels of both state capture and administrative corruption.

Figure 3.7. Foreign Direct Investment and Corruption

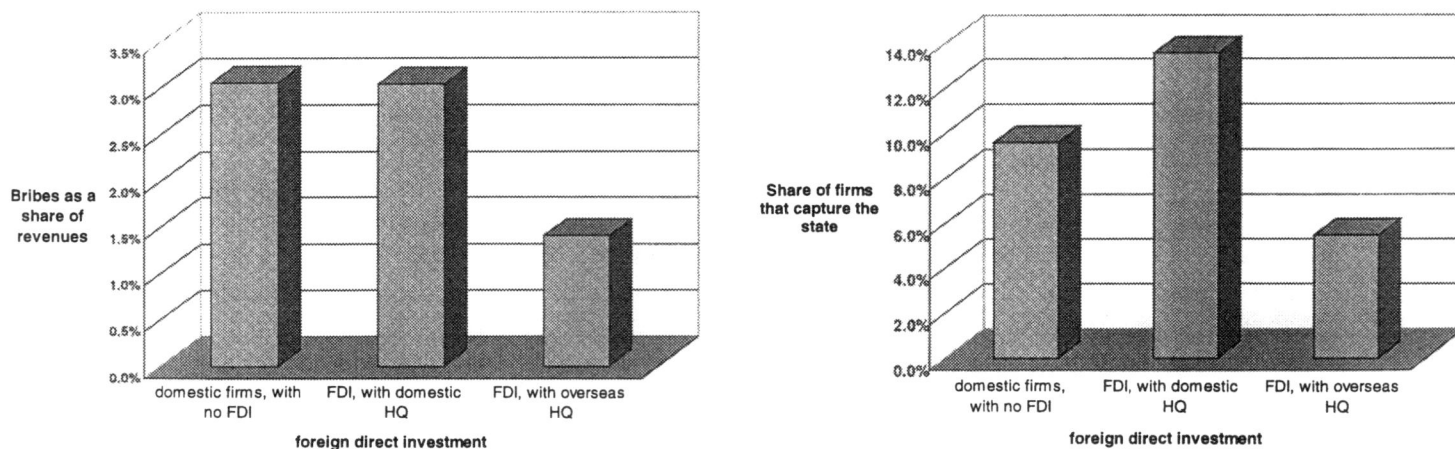

Data Source: BEEPS; Hellman, Jones, Kaufmann (2000b)

A closer inspection of these relationships within different groups of countries reveals that FDI appears to have a very different impact in different environments. Figure 3.8 shows that in countries with high levels of administrative corruption and state capture, FDI firms with domestic headquarters are substantially more likely than domestic firms to engage (or be compelled to engage) in both forms of corruption. In other countries, all forms of FDI are associated with less corruption. The negative impact of FDI in domestic firms is particularly striking in a number of high capture countries—such as Azerbaijan, Georgia, Latvia, Moldova, and Ukraine—where these firms are more than twice as likely to engage in state capture than are non-FDI firms. While foreigners might be inclined to invest in sectors and firms that are prime targets for corruption, this result raises doubts that foreign direct investment imports higher standards of corporate behavior with the ability to influence practices in high corruption settings. Many of the high-corruption countries are in the CIS, where the institutional arrangements for corporate governance are especially weak.[28] Thus, to the extent that foreign investors in companies with domestic headquarters seek to curb corrupt practices, they may not have sufficient instruments in the CIS for influencing the behavior of managers.

Figure 3.8. Foreign Direct Investment in High-corruption Countries

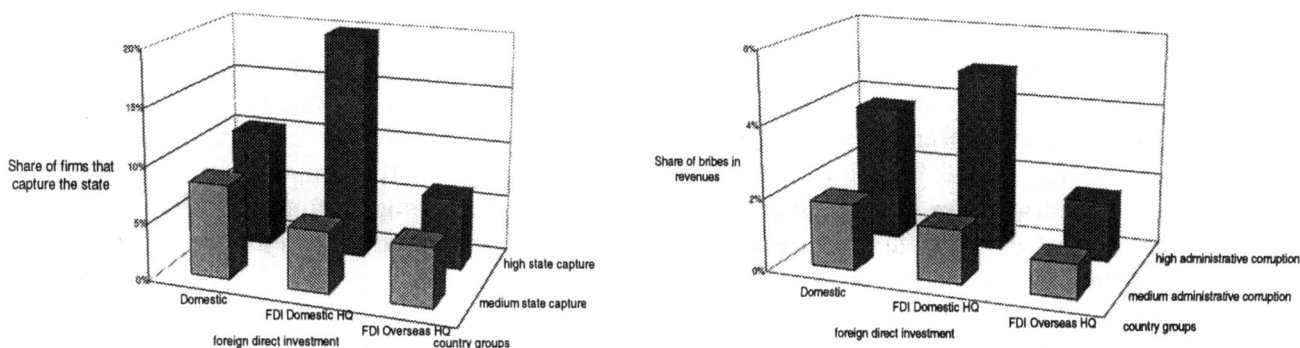

Data Source: BEEPS; Hellman, Jones, Kaufmann (2000b)

Foreign aid might be subject to similar dynamics. A recent comparison of countries worldwide (unfortunately excluding countries in transition) indicates that foreign aid can induce corruption, as competing social groups use corruption to extract benefits from this aid.[29] Countries in transition are also vulnerable to this problem, especially where institutions for public resource management are most seriously underdeveloped.

Vicious or Virtuous Circle?

The process described in this chapter suggests that institutional and economic legacies had a profound impact on initial choices of political institutions and on the pace and substance of economic reform. In countries with weak institutions and strong incentives for corruption, restraints on the abuse of public office were insufficient to check the emergence of state capture and administrative corruption. In countries with more favorable legacies, these problems are still present, but are less severe.

Figure 3.9. Variation Within and Between Sub-regions

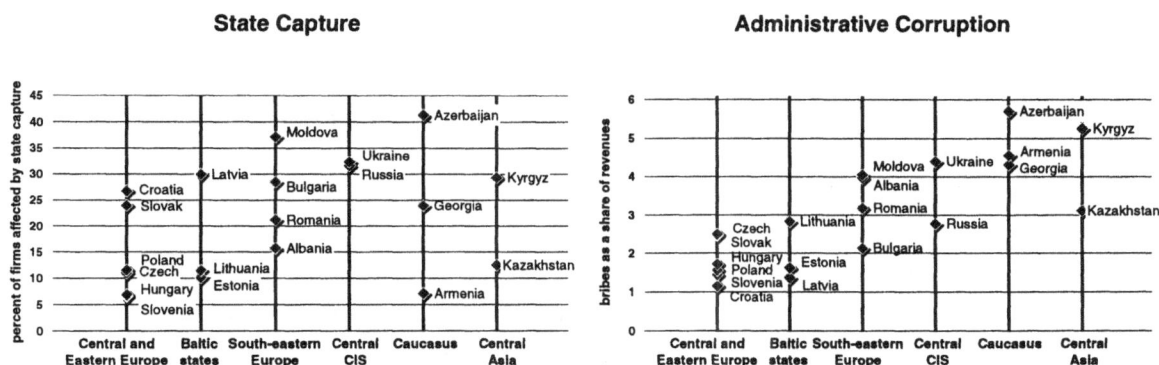

Source: BEEPS

The institutional and economic legacies inherited from the past are important for understanding current levels of state capture and administrative corruption, but this does not imply that these levels are pre-determined by such legacies. The standard geographical categorizations of transition countries actually mask wide variation in corruption levels as demonstrated in Figure 3.9. While the initial conditions discussed in this chapter explain some of this variation, a large share cannot be attributed to past legacies, suggesting that other factors, such as the rise of effective leaders and strategic policy choices, have a major impact on the nature and extent of corruption.

Yet countries can get trapped into a vicious circle, in which partial political and economic reforms become self-reinforcing. Limited reforms enable private interests both in and outside the state to shape policymaking to their personal advantage, which in turn reduces the likelihood of further structural reforms. Economies trapped in this vicious circle suffer devastating economic consequences.

The tenacity of this trap depends on the underlying incentives for reform in a country. Countries in which civil society is repressed, political competition is constrained, and institutional restraints within the state are limited generally face weak internal pressures for reform. Countries which are less reliant on foreign aid or are not candidates to join international bodies such as the EU or WTO face fewer external pressures for reform. Such countries could face a "partial reform trap" unless the political will to break the stranglehold of vested interests on the reform process is marshaled.

Can countries also become locked in a virtuous circle? We cannot emphasize too strongly that no country in transition is sufficiently developed to be immune to problems of corruption; in fact, no country in the world is immune. Even the most advanced transition countries remain at risk of backtracking as increasingly influential private sector interests seek to shape the remaining agenda of structural reform to their own advantage. Yet the proper institutional reforms and policy choices are mutually reinforcing and can have a demonstrable impact in reducing corruption levels, as a number of countries have already shown (see Chapter 6).

[1] See for example Holmes (1999) for a discussion of the effects of multiple simultaneous transitions.

[2] For example, see Mauro (1995); La Porta and others (1997, 1999); Easterly and Levine (1997); Ades and Di Tella (1999); Treisman (2000); Broadman and Recanatini (2000).

[3] Murrell, Dunn, and Korsun (1996) developed this concept to describe the process of economic liberalization in Mongolia.

[4] Underpinning this analysis is a series of firm-level regressions, in which state capture and administrative corruption are explained by firm, industry, and country characteristics. These characteristics include: (i) the size, ownership form, and age of the firm; (ii) dummy variables describing the industry of the firm and its membership in a business association; and (iii) variables measuring institutional legacies of a country, such as the natural log of the number of years it was a state in the last century, a dummy variable indicating whether it was a member of the CIS, a dummy variable indicating whether it had been part of the Habsburg Monarchy, a dummy variable indicating whether it was centrally planned (as opposed to labor managed or market socialist), an index of political liberalization at the onset of transition, an index of economic liberalization at the onset of transition, a dummy variable indicating whether it was resource-rich, and more. Generally, those variables described by the figures in the text were those that were significant and robust to many different specifications. Surprisingly, a dummy variable measuring whether a country is in the CIS was useful in explaining administrative corruption, but not state capture.

[5] The measure of experience with sovereignty is the number of years during the previous century that the country was a sovereign state. See Annex 1.

[6] See Annex 1.

[7] In contrast, countries that were formerly part of the Russian, Prussian, or Ottoman Empires do not share this legacy. Some countries, such as Poland, were formerly part of multiple empires.

[8] As explained later, deeper exploration of the relationship between democracy and corruption indicates that, while significant political reform impedes corruption, partial political reform may facilitate corruption.

[9] See Annex 1.

[10] See Annex 1.

[11] In fact, below-subsistence wages may attract a disproportionate share of dishonest workers as honest workers forgo job opportunities in the public sector.

[12] Studies of the determinants of economic policy decisions, such as the depth and speed of liberalization, clearly indicate that institutional legacies at the onset of transition have had a profound impact on policymaking. See, for example, de Melo and others (1997) and Heybey and Murrell (1999) for an analysis of the role of initial conditions on reform policy and growth.

[13] And in fact was an important European power between the twelfth and nineteenth centuries.

[14] While the particular modality of social opposition to communism was different in Hungary and Czechoslovakia, similar stories can be told about the importance of their institutional legacies in the shaping of their political structures and economic policies.

[15] See Annex 1.

[16] One important network consists of former members of the internal police, especially the KGB. See TraCCC (2000) for a summary of the role of former KGB in fostering corruption.

[17] See Rosenburg (1995) for a provocative investigation into the human rights dimension of lustration in the Czech Republic, Germany, and Poland.

[18] TraCCC (2000). Also see Wedel (2000) for a discussion of the role of informal networks in transition.

[19] This section draws on Hellman, Jones, and Kaufmann (2000a), which includes a full econometric treatment of the relationship between political and economic liberalization and state capture.

[20] Hellman (1998).

[21] Lieberman and Veimetra (1996).

[22] Holmes (1999).

[23] One study that examines this link is Kaufmann and Seigelbaum (1996).

[24] Desai and Goldberg (2000).

[25] One potential explanation for these higher standards is linked to the pressures on foreign firms from the OECD convention legal covenants—now ratified by most countries—that make transnational bribery illegal. In the case of the U.S. foreign investors, such laws predate the OECD convention by more than 20 years.

[26] Regressions of corruption on enterprise characteristics such as size, ownership, age, industry, and FDI confirm the associations between corruption and FDI depicted in Figures 3.5 and 3.6. See Hellman, Jones and Kaufmann (2000b) for a full characterization of the relationship between FDI and different forms of corruption.

[27] In this graph, the measure of state capture is the percentage of firms *actively* engaging in state capture. See Annex 1.

[28] Djankov and Murrell (2000).

[29] See Svensson (1998).

Chapter 4: A Multi-pronged Strategy for Combating Corruption

To be effective, efforts to reduce corruption must move beyond a narrow response to its immediate manifestations to a broader approach of addressing its underlying causes. The preceding chapters have demonstrated the complex mix of historical legacies, institutional factors, and policy choices that have influenced the incidence of state capture and administrative corruption across the region. Dealing with these problems will require a multi-pronged strategy tailored to the specific pattern of corruption in each specific country.

To date, anticorruption programs have largely focused on measures to address administrative corruption by reforming public administration and public finance management. But with the increasing recognition that the roots of corruption extend far beyond weaknesses in the capacity of government, the repertoire has been gradually expanding to target broader structural relationships, including the internal organization of the political system, the relationship between the state and firms, and the relationship between the state and civil society.

Figure 4.1. Multi-pronged Strategy: Addressing State Capture and Administrative Corruption

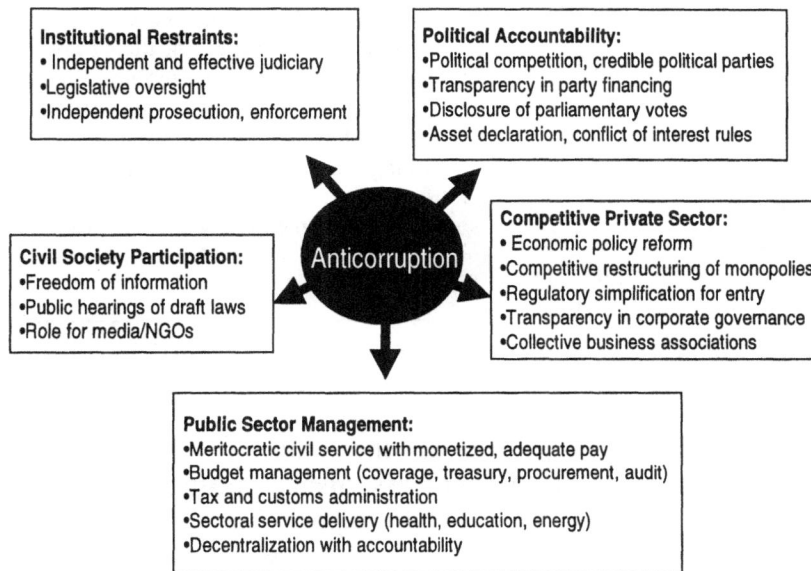

Institutional Restraints:
• Independent and effective judiciary
•Legislative oversight
•Independent prosecution, enforcement

Political Accountability:
•Political competition, credible political parties
•Transparency in party financing
•Disclosure of parliamentary votes
•Asset declaration, conflict of interest rules

Anticorruption

Civil Society Participation:
•Freedom of information
•Public hearings of draft laws
•Role for media/NGOs

Competitive Private Sector:
• Economic policy reform
•Competitive restructuring of monopolies
•Regulatory simplification for entry
•Transparency in corporate governance
•Collective business associations

Public Sector Management:
•Meritocratic civil service with monetized, adequate pay
•Budget management (coverage, treasury, procurement, audit)
•Tax and customs administration
•Sectoral service delivery (health, education, energy)
•Decentralization with accountability

Experience has demonstrated that there is no single model to determine how these relationships should be structured to minimize the risks of corruption. Indeed, a wide range of diverse models is available from contemporary practice and historical experience. Though the methods may differ across countries, the goals are the same: enhancing state capacity and public sector management, strengthening political accountability, enabling civil society, and increasing economic competition.

This chapter defines and describes five key building blocks of an anticorruption strategy, illustrated in Figure 4.1. The next chapter shows how the strategy can be tailored to countries confronting different profiles of corruption.

Increasing the Accountability of Political Leaders

The first block consists of actions that can be taken to increase political accountability. Political accountability refers to the constraints placed on the behavior of public officials by organizations and constituencies with the power to apply sanctions on them. As political accountability increases, the costs to public officials of taking decisions that benefit their private interests at the expense of the broader public interest also increase.

Accountability rests largely on the effectiveness of the sanctions and the capacity of accountability institutions to monitor the actions, decisions, and private interests of public officials. *Transparency* via public scrutiny has proven to be one of the most powerful forms of monitoring public officials. Such transparency can be fostered by a number of measures, including: opening sessions of the parliament, government, and the courts to the public; registering lobbying activities; and publishing the voting records of parliamentarians, annual reports of government bodies, trial records, and the decisions of judges. Among these, effective laws on disclosure of conflict of interest, including the receipt of gifts and other benefits received from private sources, are particularly lacking throughout the region (see Box 4.1). To be fully effective, however, such laws need oversight and implementation bodies. Public access to information on the interests of high public officials, as found in Georgia and Latvia, can reinforce the impact.

> **Box 4.1: Disclosures of Conflict of Interest**
>
> Lawmakers and policymakers in countries liable to state capture are uniquely vulnerable to conflicts of interest. Laws designed to prevent decisionmaking in a situation of conflict of interest typically require state officials to declare their assets and may also regulate the receipt of gifts by public servants. Such laws feature in many countries, including Albania, Czech Republic, Estonia, Georgia, Latvia, Lithuania, Poland, and Russia, but vary widely in the effectiveness of their implementation and in the extent to which they require public access to the information contained in declarations. Latvian law reinforces the incentives created by disclosure by penalizing illicit enrichment of officials who cannot justify possession of assets in excess of their normal sources of income. Lithuania has successfully used the asset declaration law to remove corrupt public officials from office.

Effective sanctions on politicians can be enhanced most effectively through a meaningful degree of *political competition* in the electoral process. Such competition increases the likelihood that alternative candidates and parties will seek to expose corruption in government or hold politicians accountable for the poor performance associated with high levels of corruption. The issue of corruption has been a key factor in elections across the region in such countries as Bulgaria, the Czech Republic, Latvia, and Poland, among others. However, excessive political competition can become a destabilizing factor if it leads to fragmentation of the political system or if it undermines the legitimacy of existing state institutions. This is most likely to occur when political parties are organized largely around rival ethno-linguistic groups with competing claims to the definition of the nation-state, as in Bosnia and Herzegovina. Excessive political competition can undermine state capacity and thus create conditions especially conducive to administrative corruption, but conducive to state capture as well.

Political competition is most effective in promoting accountability when it is channeled through organizations that provide broad constituencies with vehicles—such as mass-based political parties and interest groups—to express their collective demands to political leaders. While mass-based political parties are gaining credibility in CEE, in many other transition countries they remain unstable and tenuously linked to broad constituencies. This exacerbates politicians' dependence on powerful firms and financial interests—sometimes outside the country's borders—for sources of financing and on electoral tactics such as vote-rigging, intimidation, and acquiring a monopoly over election coverage by the media. It is imperative that political parties be held to the same standards of accountability as those described above. Effective, well-monitored rules on political party financing are of particular importance (see Box 4.2).

Accountability mechanisms need not be entirely based on external constituencies and competitive pressures. Indeed, in certain contexts, such mechanisms can also be created within government bureaucracies by establishing ethics codes, regulations on lobbying, disciplinary committees, prohibitions on conflict of interest, and mandatory disclosure of income and assets. Ensuring credible sanctions and effective internal monitoring of bureaucratic behavior is critical to the success of such an approach.

Strengthening Institutional Restraints

The institutional design of the state can be an important mechanism in checking corruption, in particular, the effective development of institutional restraints within the state most effectively achieved through some degree of separation of powers and establishment of cross-cutting oversight responsibilities among state institutions. Effective constraints by state institutions on each other can diminish opportunities for the abuse of power and penalize abuses if they occur. An independent and impartial judiciary is often the most important constraint, as the existence of genuine legal recourse underpins the credibility of other institutions of the state and allows these institutions to be credibly challenged when needed.

Box 4.2: Political Party Financing: Experience And Mechanisms[1]

Experience worldwide shows the immense difficulties of installing an effective system of party funding that will not be open to abuse. Many countries have experienced malpractice in public procurement that provided kickbacks for party funding, as well as a plethora of other improper channels involving state-owned enterprises, privatization, and the leverage afforded by appointments and control rights at all levels of government. However, international experience also shows that regulation of party funding can be effective if well-designed, backed by effective sanctions, and accompanied by a parallel diffusion of appropriate ethics and norms. Ultimately it is committed politicians and citizens who have asserted the principles that should govern party financing and have driven through new laws and regulations. These rules need oversight, enforcement, and monitoring. This requires reliable judges or electoral authorities and an active investigative press. In some cases, the shame—and electoral consequences—of political exposure have proved effective. There is no single prescription for success, as party financing rules have to operate in an environment of institutions and degrees of rule-respect that varies across countries, but many countries have found a selection of the following mechanisms to be helpful.

- *Leave a paper trail.* Ensure that all donations and other sources of party revenue are made public, that donors and the amounts of their donations are identified in the public record, and that candidates disclose links to lobbyists, as well as sources, types, and amounts of support, both before and after elections. Expenditures and their purposes should be similarly published and available for audit.
- *Ban the use of state resources for political purposes.* Parties in government should not use state funds, postal services, cars, computers, or other assets for political purposes or in election campaigns.
- *Limit expenditures.* Make party politics as inexpensive as possible. Usually the demand exceeds the supply of funds, leading to a search for funding that may breach legitimate frontiers. There is a lot to be said for reversing this relationship by mechanisms used in a large number of Western European and other countries: (i) allocating free time slots on TV and radio to qualifying political parties, with no additional time allocation permitted; and (ii) imposing legal limits on spending, with actual expenditures subject to audit and to effective sanctions in the case of breaches of the limits.
- *Consider public funding.* Many countries have established partial public funding, recognizing that political parties play a public interest role: they make an essential contribution to political contestability and the decentralized expression of diverse values and interests. Public funding reduces the scope for private interests to "buy influence" and can also help reinforce limits on spending, because of the electorate's resistance to excessive public expenditure.
- *Build public service neutrality.* Ensure that the public service is politically neutral and that public servants are neither allowed nor required to make contributions to political parties as a way of obtaining public sector employment. This will contribute to a meritocratic public service that will resist party bias and will encourage decisionmaking in the public interest.
- *Limit types of donors.* Some countries have outlawed donations from both public and private sector companies, such as France since 1995, or foreign donations.
- *Ensure oversight.* Set up an authoritative and independent Electoral Commission or Court to be responsible for the integrity of all issues regarding party finance and electoral rules. Such commissions have been set up in Canada, India, Ireland, and South Africa.

The institutional arrangements governing the distribution of the legislature, executive, and judiciary vary across Central Europe and the CIS. Most CIS countries have presidential or semipresidential systems, while most countries in Central Europe have parliamentary systems, within which the balance of power varies considerably. In principle, devolution of powers from the central to subnational levels of the state could also contribute to institutional restraints. But experience within the region indicates that decentralization in the absence of effective capacity and accountability often increases vulnerability to corruption. In many countries of the region, corruption at the subnational level has become a particularly serious problem.

Audit organizations can also have an important role. A good—but rare—example is Poland's Supreme Audit Chamber, which investigates and publishes reports on abuses in procurement, management of public assets, and other diversions of public funds. For full effectiveness, State Audit Offices should be backed by parliamentary committees that review and follow up on their reports. By contrast, watchdog enforcement agencies have a mixed record and have too often been subject to capture themselves. A condition for their effectiveness is the prior establishment of a core of strong, independent, and credible professionals in the judicial, prosecutorial, and police arms of the state.

A frequent complaint is favoritism of the state in cases brought by citizens. Box 4.3 describes mechanisms to prevent and resolve disputes between citizens and the state.

Box 4.3: Transparency and Recourse in Administrative Decisionmaking

Government decisions are less prone to corruption when they are predictable, transparent, and accountable. Administrative procedures law provides the legal foundation for sound government decisions by providing rules for the way government bodies behave. These procedures protect the rights of citizens by guaranteeing participation in government decisions by interested parties, openness and transparency of decisions, adequate responses to public inquiries, and the availability of recourse. Mechanisms of recourse include appeal within government bodies, judicial scrutiny, and ombudsmen. Explicit administrative procedures allow citizens who are affected by administrative decisions to know that decisions will be made according to predictable rules rather than the will of the administrator.[2]

In the context of corruption, one of the crucial differences between CEE and CIS countries involves differences in administrative procedures. Most countries in Eastern Europe possess at least basic guidelines for administrative decisionmaking and dispute resolution, unlike most in the former Soviet Union. In an attempt to strengthen public administration and protect the rights of their populations, a number of transition countries are developing their own administrative procedures. Latvia, for example, is introducing legislation to create a system of administrative courts dedicated to the adjudication of disputes between citizens and the state. The Latvian government considers the introduction of such courts to be integral to the efficiency and credibility of government decisionmaking.

Judicial systems in the region are generally considered to be capable of independent decisionmaking, although in some countries judiciaries have not yet established effective autonomy. In others, their capacity for independence is not always matched by performance, and lower courts are often managed by the Ministry of Justice with oversight provided by the procuracy.

Raising judicial credibility is a challenging task. Judicial independence is critical but must not come at the expense of accountability. Reforms specifically aimed at raising judicial accountability consist of setting and monitoring judicial performance standards and ethical behavior, introducing greater transparency in relations between judges and litigants, publishing trial records and judicial decisions, and introducing transparent methods of case assignment. Private lawyers may also play an integral role in facilitating judicial corruption, by acting as an intermediary between the judge and the litigant. The enforcement of professional behavior in the legal professions can be strengthened by professional associations that set and monitor standards for legal practice and by developing a system of consumer protection.

Budgets should be aligned with judicial functions. A mismatch between judicial functions on the one hand and judicial capacity and resources on the other has placed severe limits on the ability of the judiciary to deliver its services efficiently and honestly. Such a mismatch also creates an imbalance between demand for and supply of judicial services. In the Slovak Republic, for example, there have been serious backlogs of company registration applications and in Poland long delays are common in the registration of land transactions through underresourced courts. Few courts are specialized in commercial matters. Largely as a result of the perceived unreliability of the formal institutions, there is a disturbing trend in some countries for commercial disputes to be settled privately and occasionally by force.

Where budget stringency persists, judicial functions should be trimmed and alternative modes of delivering these functions should be explored. For example, registry functions can be assigned to special-purpose bodies; the enforcement of court decisions in the Slovak Republic, although still regulated, has been partially devolved to the private sector.

Independent prosecution remains a crucial challenge for countries in the region. Often the legal framework for anticorruption is incomplete or unclear. Because direct evidence of corrupt acts is often difficult to obtain, many countries have criminalized activities that are often associated with corruption, such as laundering proceeds from corruption and other crimes. Box 4.4 provides more detailed information on the legal framework for prosecution of money laundering cases.

Box 4.4: Anti-money Laundering

"Dirty" money is "laundered" to make it appear "clean" when illegally obtained money is transformed so that it appears to have come from legitimate sources. The series of transactions can be complex, but three basic steps are typically involved: placing the illicit cash in the banking system, layering transactions to make it difficult to trace the funds, and integrating the illicit money with money from legitimate sources.

Legislation is needed that defines money laundering, declares it a criminal offense, and designates a state authority to receive suspicious transactions reports, maintain and analyze these data, cooperate with other countries in investigations of financial crimes, and coordinate efforts with international institutions. Financial institutions should be obliged to review transactions and report suspicious activities to authorities, and to have written policies and procedures in place so that the institution can be confident its customers are not using it for the purpose of money laundering.

Some countries in transition have anti-money laundering laws in place, but few enforce them effectively. Common weaknesses include: failure to criminalize the transfer or possession of money obtained from illegal activities; failure to oblige non-bank financial institutions (such as insurance companies, securities firms, investment companies, or cambios) or businesses often used by money launderers (casinos, bookmakers, garages) to report suspicious transactions; failure to provide the legal basis for seizure of proceeds from illegal transactions; and lack of capacity and resources to enforce the law.

Strengthening Civil Society Participation[3]

As stakeholders in the quality of governance and institutions mediating between the state and the public, the organizations that comprise "civil society"—citizens groups, nongovernmental organizations, trade unions, business associations, think tanks, religious organizations—can have an important role to play in constraining corruption. Under communism, however, civil society was severely repressed. In a few cases, the power of collective will managed to overcome the repression— a strong trade union movement in Poland helped create political competition and supported social cohesion through the painful periods of reform, and civic associations were a feature of other CEE transitions. Yet such organizations were the exception; early in the transition, and even today, NGOs in many countries are still in the early stages of development or remain as appendages of the state.

More recently, there has been an emergence of greater civil society activism in the transition countries regarding corruption. Twenty-six civil society initiatives against corruption in 17 transition countries were surveyed for the purposes of this report. These grass-roots[4] initiatives demonstrate the varied role that participation by civil society can play in fighting corruption. Most of the activities have revolved around three key themes: creating public awareness about corruption; formulating and promoting action plans to fight corruption; and monitoring governments' actions and decisions in an effort to reduce corruption. (See Box 4.5 for an example.)

Box 4.5: Giving the People Voice

The People's Voice Program[5] in Ukraine aims to build integrity at the municipal level through strengthening the voice of citizen groups demanding better governance and services, and by facilitating more responsive public organizations. Through surveys, information on the problems associated with major services is gathered. This information is then used by citizen groups to put pressure from below on local leaders to improve service delivery. The project also supplies technical assistance to municipal agencies that should enable them to be more responsive. Surveys of households, enterprises, and public officials have revealed a high level of dissatisfaction with the quality of public services, while also showing that most citizens (more than 90 percent) have never filed any complaints, believing that this would be fruitless. The survey information has been widely disseminated through the media, public discussions, conferences, and through NGOs. Initial implementation results are encouraging. The municipal officials in Ternopil reacted to the survey results by creating task groups to work on the most critical problems revealed by the surveys. These groups are currently developing proposals to deal with the problems identified. An interesting initiative has emerged in the city in response to the citizens' demands— Service Centers, a one-stop shop where citizens can pay for all municipal services. The Service Centers are also proposed to be used for filing and monitoring the citizens' complaints.

To raise public awareness, organizations have often made use of country surveys on corruption, service delivery surveys, and diagnostic assessments. Seminars, conferences, and workshops have helped to publicize information about the patterns and severity of corruption and to develop action plans. These can include attempts to influence new legislation that will aid corruption control or to lobby for new institutional devices to prevent or penalize corruption. Others focus on judicial reform and freedom of information. Advocacy for legal and judicial reform, business deregulation, privatization, and procurement reform are common themes of civil society interventions. Some monitoring activities have focused on privatization plans, procurement reforms, allocation of housing, and legal reforms.

Civil society is most effective when the government treats it as an ally, rather than an enemy. In the Slovak Republic, for example, the national chapter of Transparency International was entrusted with the first draft of the National Program for the Fight Against Corruption and has regularly been invited to monitor procurements and other state decisions.

The Role of the Media[6]

Free and open media help check the level of corruption by uncovering and shedding light on abuses. The greater openness felt by the media since the fall of communism has brought with it a plethora of stories of fraud, corruption, and criminal activity, making the media perhaps the most persistent institution in the fight against corruption. Journalists have paid dearly for this: in the territory of the former Soviet Union alone, more than 200 journalists have been killed in the line of work as they investigated stories on corrupt officials or criminal gangs.[7] Though most countries of the region now have a free and open press, many factors continue to weaken the media's potentially powerful contribution to limiting corruption, including: lingering state controls; conflicts of interest generated by ownership arrangements; and corruption in the media itself. Legal guarantees to free speech form the foundation of a vibrant media. But the press may yet be inhibited in other ways, most notably by libel laws and intimidation. In Turkmenistan, the media are expressly forbidden by law from publishing any sort of criticism against another person or institution except criticism issued by the president himself. In some countries, violence against journalists has resulted in strong self-censorship.[8]

Lingering state pressure even on privately owned media is still a serious problem. In Croatia, for example, journalists who criticized the regime of former President Tudjman found themselves faced with surprise tax inspections, shut out of the national distribution monopoly, or cut off from the national airwaves.[9] Similarly, journalists in Ukraine who dig up information about public officials have reported various forms of state intimidation.[10] Government monopolies on printing, supply of paper distribution, and television signal transmissions continue in many countries, creating pressures for self-censorship.

The conflict of interest that characterized the old system of state-owned media has in many instances taken on a new form, as the business interests that are capturing the state also gain control over the media. While the news business could be a major industry with high profit prospects, the partisan nature of the ownership structure has limited its growth and development. An appropriate system of corporate governance within the media would ensure that the editorial side of the business operated separately from the business and revenue side. Allowing free entry, particularly of foreign press if it is non-partisan and competitive, can also help mitigate the problem of "media capture." Foreign investment in media in the Baltics has helped to create a highly diverse and competitive media culture. In Russia, where media organizations are often firmly aligned with concentrated business interests, a Russian language daily was recently created by foreign investors whose leading marketing angle is the newspapers' independence from the internecine battles among the so-called oligarchs.[11]

Some countries, most notably those in Central Europe and the Baltic states, have made giant strides toward creating a free press, while at the other extreme, many of the Central Asian republics and Belarus still repress the media. Freedom of the media is highest in countries with the lowest levels of administrative corruption and state capture. (See Figure 4.2[12].) A policy of openness, formalized in laws guaranteeing free access to information, strengthens tools for oversight and enlists the media as an ally in controlling corruption.

Creating a Competitive Private Sector

The transition period has witnessed a rapid concentration of economic power, while strong remnants of the state's capacity to intervene in the economy, inherited from the previous command system, have survived in many countries. The privatization process has been susceptible to manipulation by powerful state actors, enabling them to gain control of substantial parts of the economy. In many cases, monopolies were privatized in the absence of regulatory frameworks. The rapid concentration of economic power was reinforced by corruptly assigned subsidies, guarantees, directed net lending, and corporate tax arrears.

Figure 4.2. Media Repression

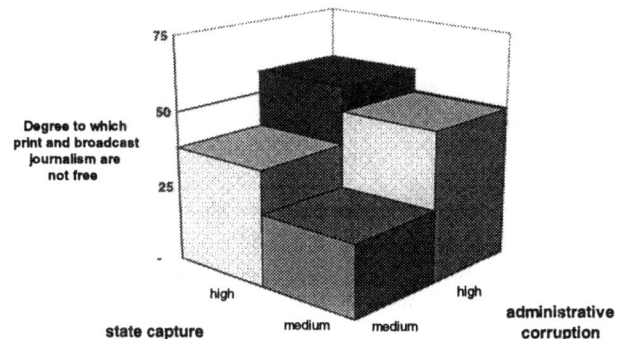

Source: BEEPS and Freedom House

Banks that were infiltrated by criminal networks are now the foundation of money laundering and other scams. Market entry has been hindered by the oppressive application of start-up rules and inspections; lack of access to bank and equity finance; and licensing and permit delays that disproportionately penalize small businesses. Inadequate mechanisms to register asset transactions foster unclear ownership structures, often masking manipulation by powerful economic and state interests. This combination of concentrated economic power and bureaucratic control has created a receptive environment for state capture and administrative corruption. Tackling this concentration of power and reducing discretionary and coercive intervention constitute the most formidable challenges of the transition, especially in light of the political constraints (see Box 4.6).

Box 4.6: Challenges of Confronting State Capture in the Energy Sector

Large infrastructure monopolies represent powerful economic interests that are able to exercise considerable influence over legislation and regulations even in cases where the scope of their activities has been formally reduced. To cite three examples:

The introduction of foreign investors to the oil sector in Kazakhstan reduced the scope of Kazakhoil's activities. Despite this, Kazakhoil remains extremely powerful and was able in 1999 to secure changes in the Petroleum Law that strengthened its own position in the industry at the expense of making the investment climate in the sector less attractive to foreign investors.

In the latter part of 1998, there was widespread speculation in Russia that international donors would push for the break-up of Gazprom as a condition of their further lending to Russia following the August 1998 financial crisis. Gazprom responded to this by securing passage through the Duma of the Gas Supply Law. This law guarantees Gazprom's right to continue to operate as a monopoly.

The Russian Government made a commitment to enact a pipeline law. Both Gazprom and Transneft have a vested interest in such a law and succeeded in pushing a draft law through a first reading of the Duma late in 1999. The draft law contains provisions that are of significant concern to foreign investors and was strongly opposed by the Ministry of Fuel and Energy. Despite this, the law passed its first reading. Gazprom subsequently realized that certain provisions in the draft law were also detrimental to its interests and with the change in the composition of the Duma following the 1999 Russian elections, the law was taken back to the drawing board.

The ability of powerful economic interests to capture the state can be constrained by: (i) economic policy *liberalization;* (ii) introducing greater *competition,* especially in concentrated sectors, by lowering barriers to entry, requiring competitive restructuring, and clarifying ownership structures; (iii) *regulatory reform* at all levels; (iv) a stronger and more transparent framework for *corporate governance;* (v) instruments of *voice* for business associations, trade unions, and concerned parties; and (vi) *transnational cooperation.*

Economic Policy Reform.[13] Although significant increases in economic liberalization have occurred since the onset of transition, many countries still have not significantly deregulated prices or other aspects of production or trade. For example, in Russia and Belarus, prices are controlled for several important product categories and public procurement at nonmarket prices remains substantial. Implicit price subsidies, in the form of tax and utility arrears, are commonplace in countries such as Georgia, Moldova, and Azerbaijan. Such interventions provide politicians and bureaucrats with discretionary power that is highly subject to abuse. Liberalization can help to reduce this discretionary power, but only if reform is undertaken in a transparent and nondiscriminatory way; otherwise, there is a risk that the reform process itself will be corrupted.

Enhancing Competition. Transparency in formulating and implementing economic policy is crucial to combating corruption, especially in the areas of privatization and regulation. Most of the state assets that remain to be privatized are large and many are in the natural resource or infrastructure sectors. Competitive restructuring of these firms prior to privatization on a case-by-case basis can reduce possibilities for corruption, although political obstacles can impede this process. Competent agencies to administer law on competition policy, antimonopoly laws, and unfair trade practices can also help. Competition can also be strengthened by introducing greater transparency in the ownership structure and operations of firms and banks, through requirements on financial disclosure and arm's-length relationships, efficient registries, and better supervision of their operations by independent regulatory bodies.

Regulatory Reform. Proper regulation of utility companies and other industries in which competition remains imperfect is important to reducing corruption. The establishment of independent regulatory agencies, both at the central and at the local level where regulatory capture is most pronounced, can be effective in promoting efficiency and limiting opportunities for corruption, as long as such institutions operate with transparency (public hearings), simplicity (well defined, rules-based principles), and accountability (election of regulators or term limitations). Similar practices for regulating more routine aspects of business operations, such as registration (one-stop registration) and workplace safety (simple and clear rules for site inspections), are crucial to limiting harassment of businesses by bureaucrats and promoting new entry and growth. For all types of regulation, firms should be provided with low-cost methods of disputing administrative decisions. Box 4.7 outlines the different approaches to business regulation that have been utilized in three of the most successful of the transition countries.

Box 4.7: Regulatory Reform in Hungary, Poland, and the Czech Republic

The experience of Hungary, Poland, and the Czech Republic in reforming their economic regulations demonstrates that improved regulatory performance is not exclusively a function of reducing the number of regulations in force. Clear rules defining when government intervention is appropriate as well as improvements in the quality of regulatory instruments are critical in establishing effective regulations that are enforced in accordance with the rule of law.

Hungary has focused on improving the quality of its regulations and on eliminating unnecessary regulations.[14] Although nearly two-thirds of its firms are still required to obtain licenses in order to operate, the government ranks high in the quality of its operations, placing first out of 20 transition countries in the EBRD Governance Index. While Hungarian entrepreneurs display confidence about their relationship with government officials (only one-quarter of firms doubt the security of their property rights), ensuring the transparent and consistent application of official requirements will remain a critical challenge in the coming years, especially as functions shift to local governments.

Poland's efforts to improve its regulatory environment have focused on establishing explicit rules to define when economic regulation is appropriate. The first step to reduce the role of government was taken in 1988 with passage of a liberal Law on Economic Activity. Over the next ten years, the absence of clear principles or criteria to guide government intervention led to the gradual but steady growth of licensing and permits requirements. By 1997, permit and licensing procedures were identified by entrepreneurs as the greatest obstacles to business operations.[15] Poland's leadership in the region in terms of private sector expansion and public sector contraction was being subtly undermined. With the second Law of Economic Activity, passed in 1999, the parliament has now sharply reduced the number of activities subject to licensing and created a comprehensive approach to licensing and permit requirements. Poland now faces the challenge of adapting its rules for creating and implementing regulations to bring them into accordance with its enacted regulatory principles. Distortions at the subnational government level in the implementation of licensing and permit rules, especially relating to land and construction, will also need to be tackled.

The Czech Republic began the transition period with a deep ideological commitment to giving free rein to market forces. The government sought to remove or limit regulations even in those areas where government involvement is usually seen as essential, such as in the securities market. In response to repeated crises, the present government is defining a more activist role for government, but little attention has been given to improving regulatory quality or to creating clear principles concerning government intervention in the economy. Regulatory expansion is occurring without sufficient attention to enhancing transparency and accountability. The problems caused by the successive approaches to regulation are evident: fully 50 percent of respondents doubt the security of their property rights and entrepreneurs believe that crime and corruption are their most serious obstacles. The Czech Republic's current predicament demonstrates that regulatory reform requires the creation of effective regulatory institutions and a framework of market rules as much as it requires the elimination of unnecessary rules.

Corporate Governance.[16] Weak institutions for corporate governance not only result in inefficiency, they encourage corruption. Poorly governed managers often use their positions to extract favors from the state which they can later expropriate, rather than reinvest into restructuring their own firms, to avoid sharing their gains with other stakeholders. Corrupt behavior is often difficult to detect, especially in countries where transactions are obscured through the use of barter and other money surrogates as the means of payment. A wide array of corporate governance reforms have proven effective in curbing both incentives and opportunities for corruption, including: public disclosure of share ownership and cross-holdings; strong penalties for insider trading and pyramid schemes; the appointment of outsiders to boards of directors; the introduction of regular, published independent audits of financial accounts based on standardized rules; the establishment of an effective legal framework for the exercise of creditors' rights; and the strong enforcement of ethical standards. Box 4.8 provides an example of ethics reform in firms in transition countries that was achieved through collective action within the business community.

Box 4.8: Business Ethics

Business associations in some EU-accession countries, such as the Czech, Hungarian, and Polish Business Leaders Forums, have focused on strengthening ethics codes. There have also been a number of business-led efforts in Russia to improve standards of corporate behavior. A small management consulting company in St. Petersburg, Sovereign Ventures, prepared a Declaration of Integrity in Business Conduct requiring signatory companies to adopt a "no-bribe" pledge. More than 100 companies have so far signed the Declaration. In St. Petersburg, the Association of Construction Companies has expelled nine companies for violating their rules of ethical conduct, which cover "unfair" practices such as failing to fulfill building contracts.

Business Associations. A challenge for countries in transition is to find ways in which diverse private interests can compete with one another in an open and transparent way. One mechanism, often overlooked in transition countries, is the use of collective business associations as legitimate instruments to represent collective interests in the formulation of law and policy. As shown in Figure 4.3,[17] countries in which firms can find expression in legitimate collective associations are less likely to suffer problems of capture and administrative corruption.

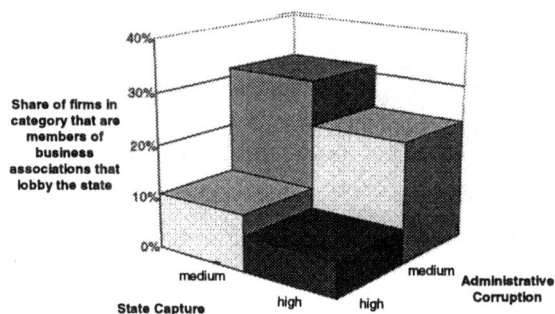

Figure 4.3. Business Associations and Corruption

Source: BEEPS

Transnational Cooperation. Foreign direct investment does not always import higher standards of corporate behavior into transition countries, especially those in which state capture and administrative corruption have already reached high levels.[18] Indeed, corruption in international trade, especially bribery of licensing and customs officials, is one of the most common and costly forms of corruption, resulting in the loss of billions of dollars each year in fiscal revenues in countries in transition. Proceeds from corruption often end up in foreign bank accounts or are laundered through foreign banks. The international community has mobilized to develop instruments against transnational corruption. As described in Box 4.9, a number of international conventions that have the aim of intensifying and harmonizing the detection and punishment of transnational corruption, and which have potential importance for countries in transition, are available for signature.

Box 4.9: International Collective Action

Council of Europe Criminal Law Convention on Corruption (European Treaty Series No. 173; http://conventions.coe.int). Open for signature on January 27, 1999, the Convention requires signatories to make the following practices criminal offenses: bribery of public officials, trading in influence, laundering of proceeds of corruption, and other common forms of corruption. The Convention also provides for the investigation and prosecution of corruption, protection of persons collaborating with investigating or prosecuting authorities, and the adoption of measures on gathering evidence and confiscating proceeds. It provides for international cooperation—mutual assistance, extradition, and the provision of information—in the investigation and prosecution of corruption. A novel element of this convention is active monitoring by the Group of States against Corruption (GRECO).

Council of Europe Civil Law Convention on Corruption. (European Treaty Series No. 174; http://conventions.coe.int). Open for signature on November 4, 1999, this Convention is the civil law counterpart of the Council of Europe's Criminal Law Convention on Corruption. It is the first attempt to define common principles and rules at an international level in the field of civil law and corruption.

The OECD Convention on Combating Bribery of Foreign Public Officials in International Business Transactions (http://www.oecd.org/daf/nocorruption). Patterned on the longstanding U.S. Foreign Corrupt Practices Act and effective on February 15, 1999, this Convention commits 34 signatory countries to adopt common rules to punish companies and individuals who engage in bribery. The Convention makes it a crime to offer, promise, or give a bribe to a foreign public official in order to obtain or retain business. A related text effectively prohibits tax deductibility for bribe payments made to foreign officials. Twenty countries have already changed their domestic laws in accordance with the Convention.

The Council of Europe Convention on Laundering, Search, Seizure and Confiscation of the Proceeds from Crime. This Convention requires parties to the agreement to ensure that domestic law permits the seizure of property and bank records or transaction documents connected with suspected criminal activity, and criminalizes the acquisition, possession, concealment, or transfer of property one suspects as being involved in criminal activity. It further obliges signatory states to enforce confiscation orders made by a court of another signatory state, and to designate a central authority responsible for the communication with, and execution of orders of, other signatory states.

The E.U. Council Directive on Prevention of the Use of the Financial System for the Purpose of Money Laundering. This Directive requires member states to stop transactions in which money laundering is suspected and obliges financial institutions in their countries to obtain identity documentation from clients before opening accounts and to provide evidence of suspicious transactions to authorities.

Reforming Public Sector Management

A fifth building block consists of reforms in the internal management of public resources and administration to reduce opportunities and incentives for corruption. Reforming public sector management and public finance requires: instilling meritocracy and adequate pay in public administration; clarifying governance structures; enhancing transparency and accountability in fiscal management; and policy reforms in sectoral service delivery. In most cases, greater public oversight can play a key role in the reform process.

In part due to the legacy of the *nomenklatura*, the practice of political patronage in public administration continues to be an important source of corruption in transition economies. Political patronage can be a source of accountability to the patron, but it can also undermine continuity and the development of standards, institutional values, and memory in the public sector. This opens the way to conflict of interest, misprocurement, and theft of public funds. The short-term and uncertain nature of many political appointments also decreases the time horizons of public sector workers, creating incentives for predatory behavior.

A first step in reforming public sector management is to eliminate patronage by instituting *meritocratic systems* for appointment, promotion, and performance evaluation and, where feasible, establishing an independent civil service oversight body. Poland, Latvia, and Kazakhstan are now starting down this path. In parallel it will be important to increase salaries, relate them to skill and responsibility, and regularize the extensive nonsalary benefits that provide broad scope for discretion and corruption. This applies especially to CIS countries where average monthly salaries are often less than US$30, although there are a host of *ad hoc* and uneven noncash allowances. Poland and Georgia, for example, allowed higher salaries for public servants who successfully cleared competitive examinations but fiscal and political constraints have prevented other countries from undertaking such reforms.

Review of governance and functional structures in ministries and agencies should also be a high priority. Especially in the CIS countries, administrative restructuring needs to focus on separating regulatory and economic functions. Some administrations have moved central government functions into quasi-private-sector structures. These structures blur the lines of policy direction and accountability and also create an unnecessarily large number of highly paid supervisory jobs which can serve to multiply political contacts and opportunities for pay-offs. Off-budget agency funding contributes to budget fragmentation and lack of transparency. There is also a small but important category of agencies, such as the committee on statistics, that should not be subject to political direction and whose independent functioning needs to be safeguarded.. Such agencies need statutory protection, elimination of party political appointments, professional management, and freedom from political interference.

To improve transparency and accountability in fiscal management it is crucial to *ensure full budget coverage and control*. Both CEE and CIS countries (e.g., Azerbaijan, Latvia, and Poland) divert substantial resources into off-budget accounts that typically lack oversight and transparency. These off-budget transactions take different forms, from extra-budgetary funds to lack of integration of investment planning and external financing into the budget. In the Czech Republic and several other CEE countries, a further challenge is the significant magnitude of contingent liabilities stemming from nontransparent off-budget commitments.

Another challenge is to institute the key elements of a functioning budget system that ensures accountability. *Budget formulation* is often flawed by ambiguity between executive and legislative roles, poor parliamentary processes, lack of strategic policy coordination and consultation, and inability to impose trade-offs at the executive level. Expenditure projections lack a medium term perspective and revenue forecasts are unrealistic, leading to ad hoc and nontransparent adjustments during budget execution. Expenditures on defense and internal security tend to be even less transparent and accountable than other expenditures. Unclear appropriations and unreliable disbursements often leave public managers unable to deliver reliable services. They also undermine the accountability of budget managers and undermine monitoring and evaluation. Progress is being made but it has been slow and sporadic.

Reforms to promote greater accountability and control over budgetary expenditures *require robust accounting and auditing and a strong budget execution proces*s. *Treasury systems* are crucial here, and a challenge in many CIS countries and some CEE countries is to bring the bulk of public expenditures within the accounting and reporting framework of treasury systems. Investment in information technology—seen in the treasury, accounting, and audit systems in

Russia and Kazakhstan—needs to be well grounded in broader institutional reforms. Transparent and competitive *procurement* is essential to prevent corruption from inflating public expenditure. In this context, web-based procurement can be a valuable aid to transparency.

The effectiveness of *external and internal audit* entities varies greatly. In some countries such as Kazakhstan and the Kyrgyz Republic, the external audit entity is constitutionally dominated by the executive, thus limiting its independence and credibility. To be effective in reducing corruption, external audit must be independent and equipped with strong auditing and diagnostic skills, moving beyond individual fault to target systemic weaknesses. Internal audit also needs to be developed further. Parliamentary and public oversight needs to be strengthened, with public dissemination of audit findings and scrutiny by Parliamentary Audit committees— which too often do not exist.

Corruption in *customs and tax administration* lowers state revenues, creates a distorted private sector environment, and is often linked with smuggling and organized crime. Reforms to simplify tax policy and eliminate discretionary exemptions help, as do professional staff, standardization of forms and procedures, and transparent systems such as the use of computerized risk analysis at the borders. It is important to eliminate one-on-one contact between taxpayers and officials and ensure that operating and management systems are efficient and easily monitored, including through periodic taxpayer surveys.

Finally, administrative corruption can be profoundly damaging to the level and quality of *service delivery* across key sectors. It is often deeply rooted in distorted policies, as illustrated in the energy and health sectors. Corruption, for instance, plagues the interface with customers and lies behind the low collection rates reported by many electricity, gas, and district heating companies. In Azerbaijan, the state-owned Baku Electricity Company reports a household collection rate of 12 percent despite employing 1,000 payment collectors. Sale of the distribution company (Armenia, Georgia, Moldova, Poland, and Ukraine), or privatization/management contracts (Albania, Azerbaijan, Bulgaria, Estonia, Latvia, Romania, and Russia) can help, as long as tendering and contracting processes are transparent and contract execution can be monitored. Reducing noncash transactions including barter and arrears offsets can also reduce private rent-seeking, as noncash exchange at artificially inflated rates is a standard method of extracting private gains.

Health services are characterized by interdependence of supply and demand, asymmetric information, gatekeeper power, divergence between public and private interests and incentives, and other characteristics that provide fertile ground for corruption. Patients, especially the poor, are in a uniquely weak position to counter these difficulties. Remedies include a set of reforms in health care financing, together with complementary measures to reallocate resources to priority areas, reduce waste in the health system due to malpractice in the procurement of equipment and pharmaceuticals and a variety of other abuses, and strengthen the professionalism and pay of health care personnel. Most importantly, health care systems require basic oversight and accountability (see Box 4.10).

Box 4.10: Tackling Informal Payments and Structural Reforms in the Health Sector

Informal payments in the health sector in CEE and CIS are a frequent and growing practice and an impediment to health care reform. Survey data in 1999 show that informal payments for inpatient care were about US$160 on average per visit in Kazakhstan. In the Kyrgyz Republic these payments had to be made in about 85 percent of visits. Solutions to the increasingly entrenched practice of informal payments will need to reach deeply into the structures of the sector and society:

• Governments must make clear that side payments and other "off-budget" exchanges between public employees and citizens are unacceptable and not to be tolerated. Without a clear policy framework that clarifies the government's position regarding informal payments, it is difficult for a single sector, such as health, to do so. National perceptions can also be at odds with policy in the health sector. For example, despite national policy against informal charges, the recently revised Code of Ethics of the Hungarian Medical Association does not condemn such practices, making them extremely difficult to root out.

• Existing public health systems are bloated and inefficient. In an effort to retain the largesse of the past in the face of budget constraints, there has been a bias toward maintaining past facilities without culling assets, personnel, or services to maximize resource use. The result is a high level of fixed assets alongside inadequate funding for salaries and equipment, leading to alternative sources of funding among front line providers. Closing down redundant hospital capacity and reducing overstaffing should offer the opportunity to reduce costs and raise the salaries of remaining doctors and other medical personnel. In the Czech Republic and Slovenia the number of physicians has declined somewhat (although further reductions are needed) and their earnings have exceeded or kept pace with growth in overall wages; side payments to physicians now appear less common than in the other countries in Eastern Europe. Higher earnings may offer a possible, partial solution at least in some settings. However, this is unlikely to be a solution in itself. Effective strategies could include voluntary severance pay schemes and establishment of loan funds to encourage the development of private medical practice, alongside the introduction of medical standards and disallowance of outdated medical practice by those unable to master basic skills.

• Governments need to be aware that comprehensive, free services cannot persist in a budget-constrained environment. In addition to contracting capacity and raising salaries there needs to be an acknowledgement that government cannot afford everything that is in place. This means either that the scope of services and fixed assets in use need to be reduced and/or that users be required to cover the costs of some aspects of care.

• Health systems require oversight and accountability for all providers with swift punishment for transgressors. Performance is both hard to measure and a new concept in health care. However, achieving a more affordable, fair, and equitable system requires that relative performance be assessed and that performance benchmarks be set and providers held accountable for results. Fundamental to this are use of acceptable accounting standards, procurement rules, and ex-post auditing of hospital accounts combined with tools to ensure that hospital managers comply with national policies regarding informal payments. Experience shows that the development of professional medical associations and peer review can help raise standards. Policy statements in the absence of monitoring and enforcement has proven and will continue to be ineffective in reducing the prevalence of informal payments.

• Private services are increasingly being seen as alternatives. The weakness of public health services has led to a search for alternative care, but much of the "private care" is currently either financed partly by government or uses public infrastructure and equipment to treat private patients. For many countries, especially the poorest, rationalizing and raising standards in public health services will remain the highest priority. Development of genuinely private health services will require a framework to regulate and monitor the quality, reliability, and cost-effectiveness of care, determine issues relating to access, and provide transparent criteria for licensing and monitoring private health insurance funds.

Based on Lewis (2000).

Decentralization of service delivery can in principle make the state more responsive to the needs of the people and to improve service delivery. However, in countries where the accountability and capacity of subnational governments is weak and there are few safeguards against the manipulation of municipal assets and enterprises for the private gain of local officials, decentralization can actually increase corruption, bias resource allocation, and adversely affect access and quality in basic social services. This has occurred in parts of Central Asia, the Caucasus, and Baltics. In many CIS countries, improving accountability at the local level for local expenditures and to the central government in cases where expenditures are only administered by the local level (deconcentration) is a necessary first step. Reform efforts should strongly focus on creating regional/local capacity in financial management and auditing, before (or while) the decentralization process gets underway.

In parallel with reforms in sector policy and institutions, strengthening public oversight over the quality of service delivery can promote improvements in certain contexts. In Armenia, Latvia, and Albania, civil society groups have initiated periodic *user surveys* of service delivery, published findings, and ranked public entities according to their efficiency, integrity, and adherence to service standards. This has provided a powerful impetus for internal reorganization to realize efficiency gains, develop performance standards, and sow the seeds of transformation from a command and control orientation to one of service delivery and accountability.

The Multi-pronged Approach

Taken together, the five building blocks of a multi-pronged approach to combating corruption might appear overwhelming as they entail significant changes in the structure of existing economic and political institutions, in the nexus of relationships within the state and between state and society, and in the existing policy practices of governments. No government has the capacity to simultaneously pursue reforms in all these areas. Moreover, in the transition countries, the legacies of communism, the underdevelopment of public administration, and the political constraints holding back reform heighten the magnitude of the challenges.

To be effective, a multi-pronged approach requires some guidelines for the selection and sequencing of reform priorities tailored to the particular contours of the corruption problem in each country. Feasible entry points need to be identified. Coalitions of support for anticorruption efforts need to be assembled. A strategy of operationalizing reforms needs to be developed. These issues are addressed in the following chapters.

---

[1] The box on political party financing is based on: De Winter (1999), Kaid and Holtz-Bacha (1995), King (2000), Pujas and Rhodes (1999), and Rhodes (1997).

[2] Galligan and Smilov (1999).

[3] This section is based on Paul (1999).

[4] Although home-grown, many received donor support.

[5] The project is supported by the World Bank and by the Canadian International Development Agency.

[6] This section is based largely on Nelson and others (1999).

[7] The Glasnost Defense Foundation (www.gdf.ru) maintains a *Memorial Book* containing the names of 209 news people who lost their lives performing their professional duties. Cited in Nelson and others (1999).

[8] McCormack (1999).

[9] Nelson and others (1999), p. 8.

[10] Nelson and others (1999), p. 8.

[11] Dow Jones & Co., publishers of the *Wall Street Journal,* and the Pearson Group, publishers of the *Financial Times,* teamed up with *Moscow News* to create the new daily in 1999. Nelson (2000).

[12] See Annex 1.

[13] This section draws heavily from Broadman and Recanatini (2000).

[14] As determined by the recent EBRD Business Environment and Enterprise Performance Survey, Hungary has one of the most active governments, ranking 3rd (out of 20 countries) in the State Intervention Index.

[15] Ewa Balcerowicz, Leszek Balcerowicz, Iraj Hashi, eds., "Barriers to Entry and Growth of Private Companies in Poland, the Czech Republic, Hungary, Albania and Lithuania," CASE Reports No. 14, 1999.

[16] This section draws heavily from Broadman and Recanatini (2000).

[17] See Annex 1.

[18] See Hellman, Jones and Kaufmann (2000b).

Chapter 5: Designing Effective Anticorruption Strategies

The previous chapter presented a comprehensive set of instruments for combating corruption. The challenge remains to draw lessons from the typology of corruption for prioritizing, sequencing, and combining reforms to design the most effective strategy for the particular contours of the problem in different countries. By unbundling corruption, the goal is to develop more effective targeting of anticorruption measures to strike at the main sources of the *persistence* of corruption. Differentiating the causes and consequences of corruption across countries should help to set priorities, to identify and evaluate opportunities for entry into serious anticorruption work, and to develop more realistic expectations regarding the necessary time horizon of reforms in different contexts. At the same time, designing an effective anticorruption strategy will always depend upon a detailed understanding of the particular nature of the political, economic, and social landscape in each country which goes well beyond the simple typology presented in this report. This landscape will strongly condition the extent to which different types of instruments will work effectively.

Referring back to the typology presented in Figure 1.5, lessons are identified for each category of the matrix and illustrated by a box on a particular country which is illustrative of the dynamics suggested by the typology. A key argument embedded in the typology is that an anticorruption strategy should be designed not only in response to the *level* of either state capture or administrative corruption alone in a given country, but to the *interaction* of these forms of corruption as well. Strategies to reduce administrative corruption, for example, need to take into account the extent of state capture, since the latter may seriously blunt the effectiveness of conventional anticorruption tools. An effective strategy for fighting corruption should recognize how the interaction of different forms of corruption enables or limits the state's capacity to implement necessary reforms.

The typology presents a static picture of the pattern of corruption across transition countries at a single point in time, but it must be recognized that the pattern of corruption is much more dynamic. Indeed, in designing an effective anticorruption strategy, it might be more useful to know in which direction a country is moving within the typology rather than its position at any given time. The typology does not set out a simple linear path of development. Rather, countries can zigzag, progressing on one dimension of corruption, falling behind on the other, or moving ahead on both fronts simultaneously. Steps backward are just as likely as steps forward. Even in the most advanced countries, the unfinished agenda of structural reform threatens to exacerbate the problem of state capture. Political regime changes could also cause an abrupt turn for the better (or for the worse) in particular patterns of corruption. As a result, describing the potential pathways within the typology as a whole is as important as describing the country characteristics within each individual category of the matrix.

The typology is presented as an *heuristic device* designed to enhance our analysis of the different patterns of corruption and draw lessons for framing effective anticorruption strategies. It intentionally strives to sharpen boundaries that, in reality, are often far more ambiguous and complex. As a result, those designing anticorruption strategies will need to examine the relevance of different categories of the typology for each country based on more information than can be provided in these simple cross-country measures. In this sense, the typology is intended as a framework for *self-assessment* of corruption within each country rather than as a device for providing a fixed reform blueprint for each country in the region. At the country level, a much further unbundling of the actual practices of and relationships behind administrative corruption and state capture will be required in order to develop and operationalize an effective anticorruption strategy.

Medium State Capture/Medium Administrative Corruption

Medium / Medium

Medium State Capture / Medium Administrative Corruption

high medium medium — high

administrative corruption

state capture

Key Focus: Capitalizing on favorable conditions for strengthening political accountability and transparency through further institutional reforms

Challenges
- Risk of complacency and backstepping
- Close ties between economic interests and political institutions
- Cronyism and conflict of interest in public sector appointments

Priorities
- Promote further reforms in civil service, public finance, procurement, and judiciary
- Introduce greater transparency into political financing
- Develop strong partnerships with civil society

Though the countries within this group exhibit lower levels of state capture and administrative corruption relative to other transition economies, these problems are by no means resolved in any of these countries. As civil society and the independent media tend to be more developed in this group, there may be greater exposure and hence greater public recognition of these problems than in other countries that have higher levels of corruption. The political consequences of corruption are not necessarily correlated with the level of corruption. Where political competition is robust and the electorate increasingly sophisticated, complacency in the face of state capture and administrative corruption has the potential to generate even greater political instability than it does in less advanced, but more corrupt systems. High-level corruption scandals, mostly linked to evidence of state capture, have been more likely to bring down governments in this group of countries than in any of the other groups in the typology.

The corruption challenges faced by these countries are still substantial, both in terms of state capture and administrative corruption. More robust political competition has not eliminated the serious gaps in such areas as financial disclosure and transparency of the political process.

More direct forms of capture by private payments to public officials have often been replaced by more discreet, though no less illicit, forms of political party financing. Legislation regulating this area is poorly developed and weakly enforced in all of these countries (as in many of the advanced countries of the world). They remain saddled with bureaucracies that retain considerable discretionary powers to intervene in the market economy. Corruption in public service delivery continues to be a particularly serious problem.

What distinguishes these countries is not the modesty of the corruption challenges they face, but the level of development of many of the key institutions and tools necessary to confront these challenges. These include civil society institutions that are beginning to grow in strength, a vigorous independent media, an evolving system of institutional restraints within the state, functioning (if not well-developed) institutions of public administration, and some foundation for the rule of law. Such institutions are necessary to build and empower the domestic constituencies that generate sustained demand for combating corruption. They can provide the critical tools of public monitoring and accountability that are essential for placing constraints on politicians and bureaucrats. They also underpin a degree of state capacity that enables politicians to assert greater control within public bureaucracies, if they choose to do so. These institutions are the essential pressure points and tools to reduce both administrative corruption and state capture.

In many of these countries—Poland, in particular—successful economic reforms have spurred a vibrant sector of small and medium-sized enterprises (SMEs) and foreign direct investment that can weaken the concentration of economic interests promoting state capture.[1] Indeed, competition and market entry can be the most effective means of reducing the economic rents that underlie state capture.

Yet, even with many of the key constituencies, institutions, and tools to combat corruption, most countries in this group continue to lack one or more of the following essential ingredients for an effective anticorruption strategy: political will; collective action; and relevant technical knowledge and practical experience.

The lack of political will or inability to create an anticorruption coalition, especially at the highest levels of the political system, have proven to be among the most serious risks to an effective anticorruption strategy. Political leaders unwilling to kickstart anticorruption efforts by starting to tackle corruption at the very top breed further complacency at all levels of the state. Weak collective action from civil society often underscores the complacency of political leaders to move forward on the remaining economic and political reforms.

While insufficient means and incentives for collective action from civil society are problems in almost all countries,[2] the challenges are compounded in Eastern Europe by widespread cynicism among the population and a profound lack of trust in the state, even among the most advanced countries of the region.[3] Whether these traits are a legacy of the communist system or a byproduct of the turbulence and uncertainty of transition, they weaken the pressure that civil society can place on politicians and bureaucrats to address administrative corruption and state capture and attenuate the mechanisms of monitoring and accountability that are crucial constraints on both problems.

Finally, even well intentioned efforts in these countries to launch an anticorruption program can quickly run aground due to insufficient practical experience and technical expertise to combat corruption. The lessons of historical experience—both positive and negative—have still not been widely disseminated across the region.

Reducing state capture requires a strategy that goes beyond the classic technocratic approach. While relatively robust economic and political competition place some constraints on state capture in these countries, there are still vast areas open to abuse, in particular political party financing and conflicts of interest. Clear guidelines on financing political parties and mechanisms to enhance transparency are absolutely essential to channel a key conduit for informal political influence into more open and competitive forms of political lobbying. The introduction—and effective implementation—of clear and comprehensive conflict of interest legislation could also have a powerful impact. Both areas require stronger verification and audit powers and further judicial and prosecutorial training and reform, worthy areas of institutional development in their own right. Strengthening enforcement mechanisms is also a feasible strategy in countries with a stronger framework for the rule of law.

These political leadership and judicial and prosecutorial reforms are needed to back up what might be called the "traditional approach" to combating administrative corruption. This approach revolves around the introduction of best-practice technocratic reforms and knowledge transfers through international partnerships in the critical areas of public administration and public finance. Elements of such an approach do have the highest chances of success in this group of countries. Priority should be given to civil service reform, where enhancing training and compensation levels could decrease incentives for corruption among bureaucrats. Implementing advanced systems of transparent fiscal management and public procurement administration could also have a potentially high pay-off for reducing administrative corruption. These reforms should be well targeted, backed by relevant practical experience, and launched with strong local support and participation, where feasible. External actors can serve as partners by helping to provide focus to anticorruption strategies, enhancing collective action among domestic actors, and providing technical assistance based on international experience, where appropriate.

EU accession can play a major role in pushing these countries toward greater progress. An active accession agenda can prevent political complacency and generate political will, even as the reform agenda begins to lose some of its urgency. Technical assistance can also provide the know-how and partnership to move forward in the most difficult areas of governance. Nevertheless, experience has already shown that the prospects of EU accession are no uniform guarantee for all potential candidates of continued progress in structural or anticorruption reforms.

Despite their many advantages, failure to act decisively to control state capture in these countries could run the risk of slipping backwards within the framework of the typology. Indeed, the most likely path of regression in countries with reasonably stronger traditions of public administration is towards higher levels of state capture. As these economies grow, the capacity of powerful economic interests to influence fast-developing legal, legislative, and regulatory frameworks could outpace the constraints imposed by competing interest groups and civil society. The risk increases in those countries where a major agenda of structural reforms remains to be completed. The case of the Czech Republic, where a once widely praised mass privatization program was partly undermined by the ability of powerful banks and investment funds to prevent post-privatization reforms, has been a prominent example of such risks. Further measures to strengthen political transparency and accountability and to enhance economic competition are necessary to check the power of emerging commercial, financial, and industrial groups.

Box 5.1: Poland

Poland has many of the ingredients for a successful anti-corruption strategy—cross-party leadership, vibrant media, and strong sources of pressure from able NGOs and academic institutes that supply analysis and advocacy. With a few prime exceptions—such as adequate laws on political party financing and rules to constrain lobbying—many of the laws needed already exist. Further ingredients needed are commitment to transparent implementation, together with sustained reform of parliamentary, judicial, and prosecutorial agencies and the public administration. As yet, strategic direction and focus, which the newly formed High Level Group may be able to bring, are somewhat lacking.

The Minister of Justice launched a Clean Hands campaign in 1994, but effective implementation did not materialize. More recently, Parliament has set up ethics and disciplinary committees and the Parliamentary Committee on Internal Affairs has published a report on corruption focusing primarily on enforcement issues. The Supreme Audit Chamber has supplied sustained leadership with a plethora of highly critical reports but with little follow-up from parliament, government, or prosecutors. Several regional governors are attempting anticorruption campaigns, with mixed success. A small number of key politicians keep anticorruption issues in the public eye, bolstered by a continuing flood of newspaper articles and television programs.

Reforms such as the recent Law on Economic Activity are intended to reduce the opportunities for corruption at the interface between public and private sectors. The new Civil Service Law is designed to combat the politicization of appointments and build a career civil service of integrity. If these laws can be successfully implemented, they will go far to lift the burden of corruption from the private sector and strengthen state institutions against corruption. A law on political party financing now on the drawing board promises to make inroads into state capture, as would effective implementation of the existing law on conflict of interest and financial disclosure.

Despite Poland's strong commitment to state-building and the market economy, close links between economic interests and political institutions continue. A particularly damaging feature is cronyism and conflict of interest in appointments to regulatory authorities, boards of privatization commissions, state-owned enterprises, and extra-budgetary funds. Public service appointments are also highly politicized, exposing some appointees to a corruption levy as well as inflicting loss of expertise and institutional memory in the poorly paid administration. High-level corruption is also manifest in interference in customs and in the award of tax exemptions, concessions and licenses, and malpractice in public procurement. Administrative corruption at the subnational government level remains problematic, particularly in transactions involving land and assets and in procurement. The health services are marred by procurement abuse, corruption at the interface between hospitals, doctors, and the pharmaceutical industry, and extraction of informal payments. The deep distrust of the state that characterized the Soviet period continues to weaken the credibility of anticorruption efforts.

Based on Sutch, Wojciechowicz, and Dybula (2000).

Medium State Capture/High Administrative Corruption

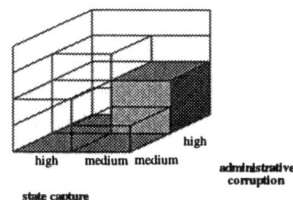

Medium / High
Medium State Capture / High Administrative Corruption

Key Focus: Enhancing state capacity to improve the provision of basic public goods.

Challenges
- Highly underdeveloped public administration
- Lack of control and accountability within the state
- Nascent civil society

Priorities
- Build the capacity of public administration
- Develop instruments for financial management
- Encourage civil society development

The key feature of most of the countries falling into this category is the weak capacity of existing state institutions, both in terms of the provision of basic public services and regulatory functions and the existing mechanisms of accountability and control within the state apparatus. In extreme cases, civil unrest or war has threatened the state, such as in Albania and Armenia. Administrative corruption thrives in such an environment and often reaches the highest levels of the political system. At the same time, corruption at the household level can be particularly problematic, affecting the delivery of most public services.

In such countries, anticorruption efforts should be synonymous with fundamental state-building. This entails, first and foremost, developing the capacity of the state to deliver basic public goods, such as public order and stability, health care and social protection, and simple systems of public revenue management. Enhancing the capacity of basic institutions of public administration and the civil service is necessary, but this should be combined with liberalizing measures to reduce bureaucratic discretion in the economy.

State capture by firms as measured by the BEEPS survey does not appear to have reached the highest levels in comparison with other transition countries. However, this may be due not to any greater degree of constraints on state actors (as in the group of countries discussed above), but to a less concentrated economic structure (such as a predominantly agricultural economy) or to the overall lack of state capacity to intervene in the economy. There are also other forms of state capture, such as by public officials themselves or by specialized state sectors (e.g., the military) that may be relevant in individual cases, but are not measured in the BEEPS survey.

In Kazakhstan, for instance, corruption appears to be relatively higher in a small number of high-revenue sectors, though not a general issue confronting all firms across the board. As the state capture index in the survey measures the proportion of firms affected by state capture, the score is relatively lower than in other transition economies. Moreover in Kazakhstan, regional and local officials are directly negotiating with firms. These actions do not involve sale of laws, are characterized by greater predictability and certainty (which also lowers the frequency and amounts of bribes that firms have to pay), and entail minimal high-level micromanagement of day-to-day administration. As a result, firms are less likely to try to buy laws, decrees, and regulations at the highest levels of the political system, accounting for the relatively lower level of measured state capture.

Civil society in these countries may be particularly weak; clans or other informal ties can lead to social fragmentation in some cases. Consequently, there are unlikely to be strong social constituencies to demand and sustain an anticorruption program. The knowledge gaps on the causes and consequences of corruption, as well as on strategies to combat the problem, can be wide. Public education and awareness are particularly critical elements of any anticorruption strategy in these countries, as the constituencies for reform within civil society are unlikely to have the capacity to sustain the demand side for anticorruption activities.

Political will to combat corruption is most likely to be driven by external pressures, especially international donors. Donors tend to play an important role in these countries, assisting in the process of state-building. Creating safeguards to ensure and monitor effective delivery of donor assistance is likely to be a priority in some countries and could be an important entry point toward a program of further institutional reforms. (See Box 5.2 on Albania and Box 5.3 on post-conflict environments.) Yet such a program should have clearly defined and limited goals, as the task of state-building will have a long time horizon.

Perhaps one of the most serious problems in this group of countries is the looming threat of higher levels of state capture. Indeed, the risk of moving toward the "high-high" category in the typology would appear to be greater than the likelihood of progress toward the "medium-medium" category described above. As the private economy develops and gathers strength, there will be strong incentives for these actors to engage in state capture. Paradoxically, stability could carry greater risks of state capture by private firms, as the influence of other important constituencies, such as the military, begins to subside.

If economic reforms move forward in these countries, it will become critical to incorporate measures to ensure competition and weaken potential vested interests in order to prevent state capture from developing into a serious challenge.

Box 5.2: Albania

Albania was one of the most isolated countries in the world and certainly within Europe during the communist period. It also remains the poorest country in Europe. Located in close proximity to Italy and Greece, expectations were high after the country opened up in the early 1990s, and with substantial external assistance, a quick transformation into an open economic system took place. However, public institutions and oversight mechanisms could not keep pace. Civil society, including the private sector community and the press, was extremely underdeveloped and authority remained highly concentrated. Simultaneously, progress in putting in place institutional restraints in the political system and ensuring judicial independence has been moving ahead, but very gradually.

The close proximity to Europe generated donor support but created problems as well. Weak state structures allowed criminal activity to flourish, using Albania as a transit platform to reach Europe. The collapse of the pyramid schemes in 1997—after they had enriched many high-level political figures—wiped out the life savings of the poorest Albanians, led to major civil disturbances, and cemented the public's distrust toward public institutions. A vicious cycle has emerged in which corruption acts as both a cause and a consequence of a chronically weak state and weak public institutions.

Following the 1997 disturbances, a newly elected government launched an anticorruption initiative with donor support. Surveys of public officials, enterprises, and households and a comprehensive government anticorruption action program were developed and presented in a public workshop in mid-1998. The surveys were instrumental in raising the profile of corruption and shaping the terms of debate. Perhaps for the first time, the domestic media—which provided extensive coverage—turned to discussing institutionalized corruption rather than scandals involving individual public figures.

The government's program was broad and comprehensive, including more than 150 specific measures in the areas of economic policy, rule of law, public administration, procurement, audit, and public awareness. Implementation of many of these reforms has been driven by donors, partly because donors wanted to assure themselves that their assistance would be effectively utilized. However, this combination of reliance on foreign assistance and weak state structures has expanded the role of donors; domestic ownership and sustainability of the reforms needs careful nurturing.

Implementation of the program to date has been mixed at best, due to a variety of factors. The political leadership itself was not free from charges of corruption. The public sector was one of the only sources of patronage for the newly elected Socialist Party coalition creating political constraints on reform. There was no unbiased forum of "last resort" since enforcement agencies and the judiciary were incapable of functioning properly and were themselves burdened by allegations of corruption. Moreover, ownership of the program has diminished over time. The Prime Minister changed three times in a two-year period. Most recently, a revised Anti-Corruption Action Plan has been announced, updating the measures and improving implementation-monitoring mechanisms. However, given the experience with the first effort, skepticism has begun to set in.

On the positive side, public administration reform finally began to move forward in mid-1998, due to a combination of domestic interests and international donor pressures and assistance. Civil service reform is moving ahead and an outreach program is under way to explain the new process to public officials, local governments, and others. NGO-organized roundtables have helped to broaden the circle of those commenting on the draft law.

Other reform measures have focused on improving financial management. Computerization of the treasury, improvement of accounting procedures, improvement of budget preparation, and internal audit reform are ongoing. One of the most important areas currently being addressed is customs, the main revenue source and considered to be one of the most corrupt entities. A new customs code and implementing regulations were adopted. Customs and tax revenues are up significantly. Reforms in the judiciary and enforcement agencies, institutional in nature, are only slowly showing results.

High State Capture/Medium Administrative Corruption

High / Medium
High State Capture / Medium Administrative Corruption

Key Focus: Enhancing political accountability and promoting new entry
to take maximum advantage of a stronger legacy
of state capacity

Challenges
* High concentration of power
  by vested interests
* Weak structures for monitoring
  and accountability
* Powerful groups block further
  reforms to preserve their
  advantages

Priorities
* Broaden formal channels of
  access to the state
* Deconcentrate economic power
  through competition and entry
* Enhance oversight through
  participatory structures

Countries with high levels of state capture alongside medium levels of administrative corruption generally benefit from a historical legacy of the rule of law and well-developed public administrations associated with previous, pre-communist regimes. However, their problems with state capture are rooted in either high concentrations of economic power in key industrial sectors (such as gas and oil transit and agribusiness in Latvia) or weakly accountable political regimes built around populist or nationalist politicians with close ties to powerful enterprises (such as the first governments after independence in Croatia and the Slovak Republic). State capture can be seen as repressing the advantages that these countries have in terms of the capacity of the state and the strength of public administration. Reducing state capture could thus unblock a powerful potential for further reforms.

In these countries, the major obstacles to further progress on structural reform lie less in the weak capacity of state institutions than in the power of vested economic interests and the private interests of powerful politicians. Though basic political institutions and civil society are much more developed in this group compared with the previous one, mechanisms of accountability tend to be attenuated in these regimes. Political access for competing interest groups is often blocked. Institutional restraints within the state are generally weak. Political contestability is less robust than in countries of the medium-medium group. Consequently, conflicts of interest abound in some countries as political leaders can equate their private well-being with the country's well-being. Favored firms develop close ties to politicians and their parties, often blurring the boundaries between the party and the firm.

The major challenge in these countries is to break the political stranglehold on further progress in reform. Combating state capture should become the key focus of any anticorruption strategy. Though technocratic reforms might be useful as entry points into anticorruption work, a credible reform program should be designed to broaden formal channels of political access and to increase the accountability of political leaders to a wider range of constituencies. Encouraging the development of institutional mechanisms of political oversight and promoting transparency in party financing could also have a positive impact. Efforts to promote collective action among anticorruption constituencies and competing interest groups (such as SMEs, trade associations, and professional societies) should play an important role in an anticorruption strategy. In sequencing an anticorruption strategy, the early promotion of political reforms and partnerships with civil society has the potential to achieve a considerable impact.

At the same time, where powerful monopolies are the prime force behind state capture, emphasis should be placed on deconcentration, competitive restructuring, and reducing barriers to entry. In countries such as Latvia and the Slovak Republic, the generally fast pace of liberalization throughout the economy slowed considerably as it reached the door of some key sectors in the economy, creating rents to particular firms through anticompetitive barriers maintained through state capture. Continued progress in privatization coupled with particular attention to corporate governance standards and regulatory reform are essential for deconcentrating economic power and breaking existing networks with the state.

Box 5.3: Post-conflict Environments

Although the Cold War ended peacefully for most countries of the former Soviet bloc, some countries and regions—Tajikistan, the Caucuses, the Balkans—found themselves embroiled in civil wars and territorial conflicts as the political map of the region was redrawn. While the recommendations embodied in this report are generally applicable to all transition countries, with relevant emphases adjusted to reflect the typology of corruption in each country, the political and social dynamics in post-conflict countries pose particular challenges for reducing administrative corruption and state capture.

The real wars that erupted when the Cold War was in demise were mostly centered around ethnic or regional divisiveness, or extreme nationalism, a fact that bears directly on both our understanding of corruption and the development of strategies for post-conflict countries. First, corruption served—and in some cases continues to serve—as a vehicle diverting state assets to promote conflict and maintain power structures. Second, the strong rhetoric of nationalist regimes exploited the fears of the population and rendered corruption to be a distant concern, at best. In some cases, the hard-line approach of nationalist regimes effectively silenced government critics and civil discourse, both of which play important roles in reducing corruption.

Post-conflict countries face unusually harsh public finance challenges. Domestic revenue collection systems are highly fragile and nontransparent and inefficient expenditure practices provide fertile ground for the diversion of public resources for private use: (i) tax collection mechanisms are notoriously weak in post-conflict countries—often tax instruments need to be created, or the *ad hoc* wartime tax regimes reformed; (ii) borders have often changed (or changed hands) with conflict and remain porous in aftermath, with weak border controls; (iii) budget management is weak (or even nonexistent in "new" states) and may indeed be captured by the dominant nationalist powers; (iv) treasuries, audits, and public disclosure of financial information are often nonexistent in post-conflict settings, either because the pre-conflict structures have been destroyed, or because they never existed.

Rebuilding the physical infrastructure of war-torn economies, particularly in the Balkans, has largely relied on huge inflows of aid. The size of the investment projects and the large sums of money involved require particular emphasis on internal controls and sound financial management to ensure that *de facto* fungible resources are put to proper use and not siphoned off through corruption and waste. The Stability Pact Anti-Corruption Initiative for South East Europe[4] calls for priority measures including:

- Taking effective measures on the basis of existing relevant *international treaties and agreements*;

- Promoting *good governance*, through legal, structural, and management reforms for better transparency and accountability of public administrations, through development of institutional capacities and through establishment of high standards of public service ethics for public officials;

- Strengthening *legislation* and promoting the *rule of law*;

- Promoting *transparency and integrity in business operations*;

- Empowering *civil society and independent media* to galvanize community action and generate political commitment.

More broadly, the regional development strategy[5] prepared for the Stability Pact emphasizes the key role that development of sound institutions and governance must play in order to effectively implement regional initiatives and policies. Three key sets of institutional reforms—improvements in budget formulation and execution, improvements in public administration and civil service, and reform of legal and judicial systems—are highlighted as necessary for improving service delivery and policymaking. The strategy further outlines how robust measures of governance improvements can be used to provide governments with incentives to reform.

While the anticorruption challenge for post-conflict societies is immense, so are the stakes. In the Balkans alone, there are some 1.7 million refugees and displaced persons, and production remains at levels 25 percent below pretransition levels. Efforts to rebuild such economies will be undermined if corruption is not kept firmly in check.

It is in this group of countries that an internal change of political regime can open up the greatest opportunities for implementing a comprehensive anticorruption strategy. The legitimate transfer of power from a once firmly entrenched ruler or dominant political party holds out the possibility of breaking or otherwise reorienting the ties between established political leaders and powerful economic interests. Regime change is often accompanied by a resurgence of political competition, a strengthening of political parties, and a rejuvenation of civil society that can increase accountability pressures on the new political leadership. This creates a valuable political window of opportunity to promote an anticorruption strategy that strikes at the root causes of the problem (for further discussion of windows of opportunity, see Box 5.4)

Box 5.4: Windows of Opportunity in Croatia and the Slovak Republic

Both Croatia and the Slovak Republic entered the transition as parts of larger states that were among the more advanced in Central and Eastern Europe. The first post-independence governments in both countries were centered on the theme of nationalism and a much higher degree of concentration of political power that may have contributed to the relatively higher levels of state capture than that found in their neighbors, Slovenia and the Czech Republic. While the challenge of unraveling the systems that developed is a daunting one, recent changes of government present valuable windows of opportunity in both countries. In the Slovak Republic, the coalition that was elected in late 1998 has placed anticorruption and institutional reform high on the policy agenda, developing a comprehensive anticorruption program, passing a sweeping public administration reform, and proposing freer access to state information. A recent survey suggests that, while bringing corruption under control will take time, there is some indication that perceived levels of corruption have fallen. In Croatia, the change of power has been much more recent. The erstwhile leader's death in late 1999 and his party's defeat to moderates in the January 2000 elections have generated an atmosphere of openness that was unknown in the earlier regime. It remains to be seen whether the new government in Croatia will take advantage of the current window of opportunity to advance a proactive anticorruption agenda.

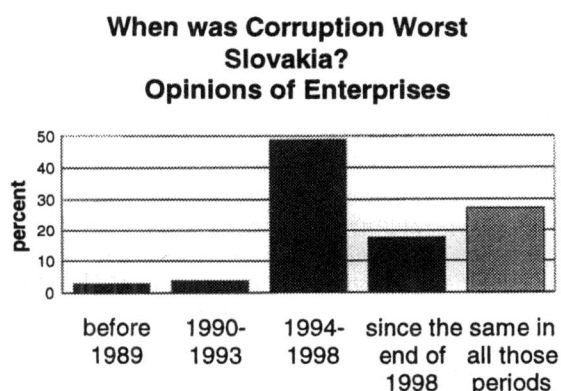

When was Corruption Worst Slovakia? Opinions of Enterprises

Source: World Bank

In the absence of a political breakthrough, continuing efforts to strengthen ties with civil society, build allies with interested anticorruption partners within the state, enhance transparency within the political system, and foster economic competition all have a potentially high pay-off by strengthening internal pressures for reform. Such measures lay a strong foundation for a credible comprehensive anticorruption strategy if the opportunity arises.

By tackling the problem of state capture, these countries have high potential to shift toward the medium-medium cell in our corruption typology, joining the other countries of Central Europe that have enjoyed similar advantages in terms of a legacy of stronger state capacity and high levels of development. Again, EU accession can play an important role in increasing the pressure to unblock the key political obstacles to further reform. Partnerships and knowledge transfers, especially to promote collective action in civil society and strengthen competing economic interests, are also essential.

However, failure to constrain and reduce state capture could lead to further regression and the erosion of existing state capacity and the control functions that have kept administrative corruption in check. The prolonged use of corrupt incentives to influence policymakers and administrators leads to diminishing confidence in public servants and state institutions. Such a low level of trust in the conduct of public officials generates further incentives to secure access by using officially proscribed means, which further weakens the accountability and legitimacy of the political system. As formal means of access decline, informal networks are strengthened to gain access to privilege. Growing informality also weakens revenue collection, limiting the resources available to build a professional civil service. As police and other enforcement agencies become clients of powerful individuals and economic interests, alternative means of recourse are sought, resulting in the use of informal and often violent means to enforce contracts and settle disputes. Consequently, state capture can eventually erode state capacity, despite favorable legacies from the past, and generate increased levels of administrative corruption as a result.

Box 5.5: Latvia

State capture is significant in Latvia, where the economy is highly concentrated, political parties are closely aligned with economic interests, and the country's position on east-west trade and energy transit routes exposes it to strong corruption pressures. Parliament's adoption in 1995 of a conflict of interest law signaled the significance of these issues. But this parliamentary initiative languished until 1997 when the Prime Minister convened the first anticorruption workshop. The effort deepened with the establishment later that year of a high-level Corruption Prevention Council (CPC) chaired by the Minister of Justice, and in early 1998 the cabinet approved a *balanced strategy* focusing on prevention, enforcement, and education. At this stage some understanding at high levels had been achieved but there was little readiness to tackle vested interests, bureaucratic inertia remained strong, and the strategy had little or no public credibility.

The Minister of State Revenue led the first stages of implementation of the new strategy, focusing on the actions needed to give teeth to the conflict of interest law and commissioning an assessment of vulnerability to corruption in Customs and the tax administration. The Minister of Finance is following up with a project designed to strengthen transparency and efficiency in management and operations. Recent taxpayer surveys indicate that taxpayer satisfaction is starting to improve—the first demonstrable results.

In a further crucial step the cabinet expanded the program outside the confines of government, releasing the strategy for public discussion at a conference in June 1998 that was broadcast throughout the country and attended by representatives of NGOs, universities, and the business community. The CPC broadened its membership to include participants from civil society and commissioned diagnostic surveys of households, businesses, and public officials.

The government is now launching a broad governance program ranging from elimination of bias in the allocation of cases to judges to infrastructure regulation to reform of pay and incentives in the public administration. The powers of the road police have been redefined. A draft law to bring financial discipline and accountability to the proliferation of public agencies is on its way through Parliament and measures to cut abuse of licensing and inspections are in the pipeline.

Despite undoubted progress under the Latvian program, the public is not satisfied by the limited improvements that it can perceive so far in public services. Public discussion focuses on the need to clean up political party financing and to implement the conflict of interest law in a more convincing way. Efforts to reduce state capture will need to complement administrative reforms if the strategy is to become fully credible and sustainable.

High State Capture/High Administrative Corruption

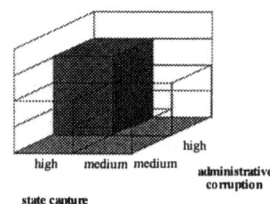

High / High
High State Capture / High Administrative Corruption

Key Focus: Breaking the hold of vested interests on the process of policy and institutional reform

Challenges
- Highly concentrated economic interests that can block reforms
- Limited implementation capacity of government
- Poorly organized anticorruption constituencies
- Restricted channels of access for countervailing interests

Priorities
- Deconcentrate economic interests through restructuring, competition and enhanced entry
- Build accountability and oversight mechanisms
- Promote collective action among countervailing interests
- Stand-alone technocratic reforms will have limited impact

Where state institutions with weak administrative capacity co-exist with a high cocentration of vested interests and a state highly susceptible to capture, the problem of corruption is particularly challenging. Powerful private interests have the capacity to block institutional reforms that would limit their capacity to extract rents from the state and eliminate market distortions that work to their advantage. The government lacks sufficient mechanisms of control and accountability throughout the state bureaucracy to implement institutional and policy reforms. Underdeveloped civil societies and intermediary associations do not yet exert sufficient pressure on politicians to counterbalance the weight of concentrated vested interests. The credibility of government on corruption issues is likely to be very low. In short, the interaction of state capture and administrative corruption makes this the most difficult environment to design an effective anticorruption program.

As the status quo benefits powerful interests, the political economy of anticorruption initiatives in these countries is particularly complex and difficult. Capture has distorted the formal and informal rules of the game to encode the advantages of particular groups into the very framework of the new institutional environment. The persistence of corruption in these countries has been supported by institutionalized incentives, networks, and relationships.

Stand-alone efforts to tackle administrative corruption through technocratic reforms in public administration and public finance are likely to have limited impact. Indeed, experience to date suggests that anticorruption strategies limited to technical reforms with fairly standard instruments have failed to produce the desired results. For example in Georgia, efforts to create enclaves of technocratic reforms in the civil service, the Ministry of Finance, and in the area of external audit have proven unsuccessful. The institutional context is as yet too weak in these countries to deliver the minimum necessary underpinnings for such reforms. Given the low level of organization of civil society and constricted formal channels of interest intermediation for countervailing social groups, such efforts are unlikely to prove sustainable over time (for an example, see Box 5.6 on Azerbaijan).

Box 5.6: Azerbaijan

Resource-rich Azerbaijan has a highly concentrated system of political power with limited institutional restraints on the executive. While the president has extensive powers, other institutions such as Parliament and civil society are relatively weak. The judiciary is not perceived to be sufficiently independent. The press and political opposition are subject to extensive controls. There is still very little separation between economic and state interests, especially in the strategically important energy sector.

In late 1998 the government began to put anticorruption on the agenda. This was seemingly due to external pressures: multilaterals and bilaterals have been increasingly withdrawing support, businesses are moving out, and levels of FDI have been less than expected. The issue has been raised in high-profile conferences and round-tables. Newspapers have started, for instance, to report on corruption (including high-level corruption). Opposition parties have become more outspoken.

In a resource-rich country like Azerbaijan, it has become obvious that a credible anticorruption strategy will first of all have to address the close ties between economic and political interests, especially in the energy sector, which afford opportunities for illicit private gains from the control of the profits and revenues. This implies the need for greater transparency in the transactions of the state oil company (SOCAR), budgetary control and transparency of revenue flows into and out of the government oil fund, and the restructuring of SOCAR itself. Several international institutions have pressed for these measures as preconditions for further support. They serve as a means to assess the credibility of the government's commitment to fighting corruption.

The government has stated its desire to embark on reform of public administration, financial management, the judiciary, and the legal system. The approach so far, however, has been piecemeal. There has been resistance to implementing stringent measures. Decreasing the powers of the Cabinet of Ministers, eliminating illicit influence in judicial and civil service appointments, reducing prosecutorial powers, and subjecting executive actions to external controls—these suggested reforms have been lightning rods for opposition from powerful and entrenched beneficiaries of the existing system.

In such environments, pursuing reforms that target state capture should also be the key priority. This requires measures on two fronts: increasing the costs to politicians of state capture and decreasing the gains to captor firms deriving from state capture. On the costs to politicians, the weakness of civil society and low level of institutional restraints within the state suggest that efforts should begin with building credible constituencies in and outside the government to bring sustainable impact. Moreover, given the low level of the state's capacity, the implementation of reforms to increase government accountability is likely to be inconsistent at best. A ray of hope in Georgia has been the work done by the agency for declaration of incomes and assets of the highest public officials, often amid adverse and financially difficult circumstances. This agency has made publicly available the declarations of more than 1,000 high public officials.

In light of the political constraints, a potentially greater impact could come from decreasing the gains from state capture to the captors. This would entail a focus on deconcentrating vested economic interests through competitive restructuring of monopolies, reducing barriers to entry, and increasing transparency in corporate governance. However, these reforms are likely to encounter substantial political resistance from those who gain from such distortions. Breaking the political stranglehold of concentrated economic interests on the reform process requires efforts to foster collective action among potential countervailing interests, such as "second-tier" companies and small- and medium-sized enterprises, to obtain political access. This could entail the development of business and trade associations and formal lobby groups to increase the range of interests with access to government, to foster competition in an effort to reduce the concentration of existing rents, and to strengthen formal and transparent channels of influence. The recent formation of the 2015 Club in Russia, which unites businesses that are committed to working together to promote higher standards of corporate behavior, is a promising development. With a greater number and diversity of economic actors competing through more open conduits of political access for a limited pool of rents, the gains from capturing the state for individual firms could be substantially reduced. In terms of sequencing reforms, these measures should be given the highest priority, especially in light of the poor initial prospects for the reform of political institutions.

In developing an anticorruption strategy in these countries, it is critical to search for a feasible entry point to break the obstacles that prevent further reforms. When the challenges are substantial and the institutions needed to deal with them are weak or compromised, finding an operational strategy that can achieve some demonstrable changes in a reasonable time frame is particularly difficult. Anticorruption programs should be designed around achievable "litmus tests" to gauge the government's commitment to reform and to recognize the limitations in such environments. Efforts to build up demonstration effects through intensive work with carefully selected organizations, sectors, or regional authorities might provide a method of entry into broader anticorruption work.

Whatever the approach, expectations should be limited and the time horizon of reform must be considered quite long. Though occasional windows of opportunity for reform might arise, it is crucial to recognize that the extent of state capture, the concentration of economic interests, and the institutional weaknesses of the state will serve as powerful constraints on the effectiveness and sustainability of reforms introduced through such windows. Unlike the countries in the high-medium category of the typology described above, windows of opportunity should not be used to introduce comprehensive anticorruption programs, since the inevitably poor implementation at later stages will undermine the already limited credibility of anticorruption efforts. Instead, opportunities should be seized wherever possible to push for the deconcentration of economic power, enhanced citizen voice, and political accountability to begin to weaken the underlying causes of state capture in these countries.

74

Box 5.7: Russia

Russia began the transition with a president and prime minister oriented towards reform, but without the institutional safeguards deriving from a strong Parliament, judiciary, civil society, and system of public administration. The gradual liberalization and de facto decentralization of property rights to incumbent managers during the era of *perestroika* and the considerable rent-seeking opportunities in the early stages of transition led to the creation of highly concentrated economic interests, especially in the natural resource and financial sectors. Partly as a result of their influence, the privatization process tended to exacerbate the concentration of power leading to the emergence of large financial-industrial groups who, in turn, have successfully lobbied the state for special privileges and opposed further reforms to create a more competitive environment. Such powerful vested interests present formidable obstacles to policy and institutional reforms that are crucial to reducing state capture, such as introducing greater entry and competition in the natural resource sector and greater transparency in government.

The challenge for Russia's new government is to find ways to break the stranglehold of these concentrated vested interests over the functioning of the state. An important first step is to reduce the power of energy producers over the state and to deal decisively with the problem of non-payments in the sector. Other important steps include introducing transparency in decisionmaking within the government and strengthening the capacity of civil society to monitor the government's behavior.

Civil society appears to be emerging as a potential force to fight corruption. The National Anticorruption Committee—an NGO chaired until recently by former Prime Minister Sergei Stepashin with formidable membership from political parties to the right, center, and left—was formed in October 1999. The Committee has begun monitoring corruption in Russia, and appears to be playing a decisive role in formulating the strategy of the Duma's Anticorruption Commission.

A number of subnational governments are undertaking systemic reforms to limit opportunities for corruption. An example of such a municipality is Obninsk, a city of 110,000. Obninsk has tried to create a transparent local government through citizen participation. With some help from external grants, Obninsk has developed a miniconstitution that declares the community's right to voice opinion. One novel example of transparency by the local government in Obninsk relates to the budget process. While developing the budget, the city administration puts the draft on an internet website. By doing so, the administration encourages comments and input from the community. Additionally, the government puts up on the internet the budget for the previous year. On a pilot basis, public goods are being procured over the internet. Not only can local administrators easily access this information, but the community is encouraged to come to city hall and use one of the general computer terminals to check up on such information as well.

Implementing an Anticorruption Strategy

Though the typology of corruption presented above provides a framework for tailoring individual anticorruption strategies to the particular pattern of corruption in different contexts, there are a number of cross-cutting principles that can be essential in operationalizing an effective strategy. They provide an operational framework for gaining a foothold to begin anticorruption work, building credibility behind an anticorruption strategy, and enhancing the sustainability of that strategy over time.

Common strategic challenges

The first challenge that all transition countries face in launching an anticorruption strategy is **credible leadership**. A serious anticorruption program cannot be imposed from the outside, but requires committed leadership from within, ideally from the highest levels of the state. Yet it is precisely the credibility of the state that is undermined by pervasive corruption, creating a potential vicious circle in which entry points for an anticorruption strategy are hard to find. Where presidents or prime ministers are unwilling to take up the challenge, leadership in strategic areas can come from a determined minister with the clout and resources to launch reforms in his or her area of responsibility or from a regional executive committed to change in a particular locality.

The second challenge is finding an appropriate **entry point** for anticorruption work. Given the magnitude of the tasks faced in most of these countries, it is critical to begin at a point where the goals are feasible and tangible results can be realized within a time frame that builds support for further reforms. Small gains can provide essential levers to sway public and official opinion. Entry points should be chosen to tackle high profile problems that respond to public opinion or business dissatisfaction.

The third challenge is to develop a detailed **diagnosis** of the nature and extent of corruption in the particular country. Experience has already shown that domestic surveys of households, firms, and public officials can be a powerful tool in any anticorruption strategy (for a more detailed description of previous experience see Box 5.8). The purpose of such an exercise is to gain essential information about the nature of the corruption beyond the general categories analyzed in this report and to identify possible entry points (see below) into effective anticorruption work. The process of implementing surveys, running workshops, and developing a dialogue within civil society on the nature of the problem can play a major role in galvanizing support for an anticorruption strategy and building constituencies at various levels of the system.

Assessment of the political culture[6] is the fourth challenge, in order to evaluate incentives and disincentives for change that will condition the feasibility of particular instruments of reform and the way they can realistically be sequenced in a particular country. Political culture relates to the way authority is exercised, and the extent to which *power* is narrowly concentrated or, alternatively, is disseminated across different institutions. It is also manifest in the way *accountability* mechanisms operate, whether through clientelism, such that the official feels accountable to a political patron or senior family member, or according to explicit rules. A further important component of political culture relates to the degree of *trust* that people feel in their institutions and in each other. Trust is also an important determinant of social capital and the capacity of communities to coordinate their efforts and act as effective participants in an anticorruption strategy.

Box 5.8: Diagnosing the Problem

One of the most vexing problems in developing an anticorruption strategy is figuring out where to begin. In many countries, gaining political momentum, generating public support and pressure for reforms, and identifying priorities have been furthered by the use of "anticorruption diagnostics." The diagnostics—at times supported by foreign and multilateral aid and at other times homegrown initiatives—include detailed surveys and public opinion polls, focus group discussions, and sectoral assessments. Diagnostics can provide a wealth of information, such as identifying the forms of corruption that officials feel are most prevalent (e.g., in the chart on Albania,[7] below) and the overall composition of unofficial payments made by enterprises (e.g., Georgia). Even in countries with relatively lower levels of administrative corruption, diagnostics show, for example, the impact that unofficial payments have on the poor and the link to small-scale business activities (e.g., Latvia), and the importance of meritocratic personnel policies (e.g., the Slovak Republic).

Common Forms of Corruption in Albania

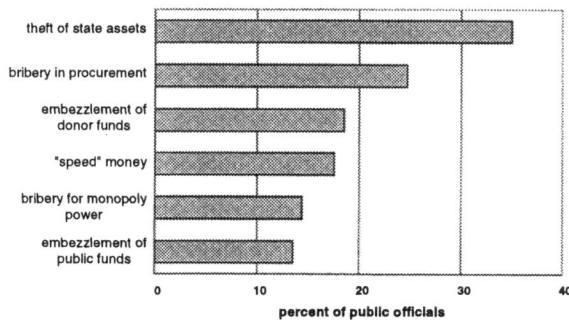

Enterprise Unofficial Payments in Georgia

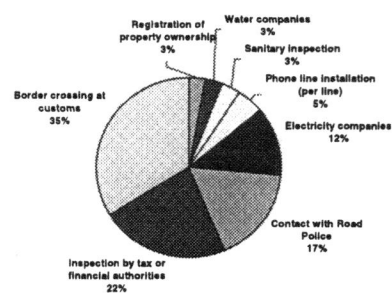

Impact on Households in Latvia

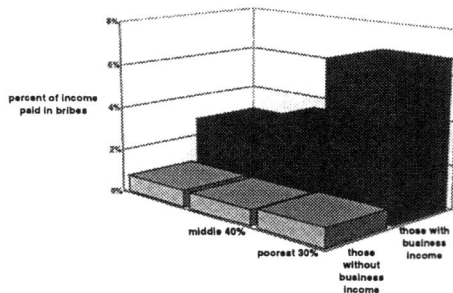

Corruption and Meritocracy in Slovakia

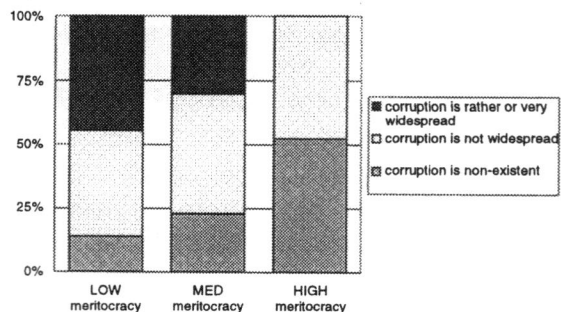

The use of diagnostics builds on the philosophy of transparency and accountability that is the key foundation for developing a sustainable anticorruption strategy. Yet, the information provided must be supplemented by other forms of expert analysis and review in order to gain a comprehensive picture of corruption in a given country.

Source: World Bank.

The final challenge is maximizing **leverage** beyond the entry point. This depends on framing reforms to appeal to the incentives influencing important actors. Efforts should be made to design "win-win" anticorruption strategies that promote the interests and reputations of major politicians and businesspeople while delivering positive externalities such as enhancing economic growth, strengthening governance, or reducing poverty and inequality.

Sequencing

There is no simple formula for the proper sequencing of anticorruption reforms. Sequencing should be developed in response to the particular constraints identified in each country. Nevertheless, proper sequencing should be designed to enhance the credibility of leadership and to ensure early tangible results to strengthen the constituency for reform along the way.

In some countries, the credibility of an anticorruption strategy may rest on the capacity of the political leadership to make an initial, highly visible, and substantive change at a high level. This acts as an indicator of commitment at the top as well as a signal for those at lower levels that their behavior must change. In other countries, efforts to tackle state capture head-on at an early stage might be impossible or even dangerous for those involved. The only possible entry points, and the only potential early wins, may be in a particular sector, such as education, which is unlikely to invoke the wrath of powerful economic interests. Yet even in these cases, measures to tackle state capture and strengthen accountability cannot be postponed too long or their absence could ultimately undermine the credibility of both the strategy and its leadership.

Throughout the region, the first impulse in anticorruption work is often to crack down on offenders without trying to tackle the more fundamental causes of corruption. Although effective enforcement must be part of any credible strategy, enforcement alone is unlikely to constitute a successful strategy. In many countries, judicial and law enforcement institutions remain part of the problem, not the source of the solution. Prosecutions can be shelved. Judicial decisions can be bought or indefinitely delayed. Police may be working for private security forces rather than the public interest. In such cases, the enforcement approach could become an instrument for repression or political victimization. Sequencing should be designed to begin to tackle the incentives and institutions that favor corruption and to educate and raise awareness of the social costs of corruption. The ultimate goal is to shift towards increased reliance on shared norms and values, instead of inadequate enforcement measures.

Sustainability

The sustainability of an anticorruption strategy depends in any context on three key dimensions. First, it requires a **critical mass of mutually reinforcing reforms** that ultimately builds into a comprehensive program. Isolated islands of integrity can provide an entry point and a valuable demonstration effect but may only survive a short time before being swamped by corruption at other levels. In order to be mutually reinforcing, the strategy must also be balanced. This suggests a mix of corruption prevention and enforcement measures combined with substantial public involvement and education to strengthen the constituencies for reform.

Second, sustainability requires the eventual development of a **broad coalition** in support of the strategy. Though gaining entry to anticorruption work might require an initially narrow approach, any strategy that relies only on high-level leadership will be vulnerable to the many uncertainties of the political process. The strategic commitment to gain entry must be broadened to incorporate key state institutions and organizations within civil society. Small- and medium-sized enterprises, professional societies, trade associations, and labor unions can all serve as important partners in an anticorruption strategy. The development of a broad coalition will reduce the vulnerability of anticorruption strategies to leadership changes and ensure that politicians ignore the corruption issues at their peril.

Where **civil society** remains severely repressed or is emerging only slowly, a combination of fear and/or lack of familiarity with civic involvement may inhibit popular participation in an anticorruption strategy. The strategy will need to include a component that can accelerate its emergence by canvassing client groups, promoting collective action, giving voice to the poor, and setting up monitoring of government services at both national and sub-national levels. External donors can play a role in funding and supporting mechanisms of voice but should ensure that they do not dominate or pre-empt the development of authentic and autonomous participation, sustainably based in the community.

Finally, sustainability requires the **resources and expertise** to see often complicated reforms through to completion over the long haul as well as deliver the credible early results noted above. This implies a mix of short-term measures and adequately funded medium-term programs that can dig deeper into the underlying causes of corruption and build institutions that can resist it. Well-intentioned reforms that are not realistically backed with sufficient resources and expertise will backfire. Governments must assign budget resources as well as competent administrators to these programs. Civil society can only do so much on its own. Business associations and NGOs can help identify priorities and can monitor results, but they cannot deploy the political will and resources of the state that ultimately are needed to reform the state and create the framework for transparent and competitive markets.

---

[1] Though it should also be acknowledged that foreign investors can also promote state capture in certain environments especially where the other institutions of accountability and transparency are still poorly developed. For a further discussion of this issues, see chapter 3.

[2] See Mancur Olson's classic study, *The Logic of Collective Action.* (1965).

[3] Surveys in the region repeatedly demonstrate this popular cynicism and lack of trust. See the many studies of Richard Rose and Christian Haeffner.

[4] "Stability Pact Anti-Corruption Initiative for South Eastern Europe—Compact," adopted at Working Table III, Sarajevo, February 15-16, 2000. Full text available at http://www.stabilitypact.org.

[5] See World Bank (2000).

[6] This section draws on Philp (2000a and 2000b), Elster, Offe, and Preuss (1998), Holmes and Roszkowski (eds, 1997)), and World Bank Report, *Making Transition Work for Everyone* (2000).

[7] The results presented in this box are from diagnostic surveys undertaken by the World Bank together with ACER (Albania), GORBI (Georgia), Latvia Facts (Latvia), and Focus and Transparency International Slovakia (the Slovak Republic). USAID cofinanced the surveys in Albania, Georgia, and the Slovak Republic. Results are provided in Kaufmann and others (1998), Anderson and others (1999), Anderson (1998), and Anderson (2000).

Chapter 6: Conclusion

Designing, sequencing, and sustaining an anticorruption program pose tremendous challenges but not impossible ones. Lessons of history and international experience suggest that countries have succeeded in addressing what had once appeared to be an intractable problem of endemic corruption. As described in Box 6.1, the United States and the United Kingdom successfully reformed their public sectors in the nineteenth century. A number of countries in Latin America have successfully undertaken initial reforms, which could grow into more comprehensive programs. Evidence suggests that corruption has declined in countries such as Hong Kong and Singapore that have undertaken comprehensive and well-targeted reforms. These success stories demonstrate that progress comes slowly, not as a result of noisy anticorruption campaigns, but because of sustained commitment on the part of political leaders and pressure from society.

Figure 6.1. Change in the Extent of Bribery During the Last 5 Years

(The View of the Firm, GCS/WEF, 1998, Selected Countries)

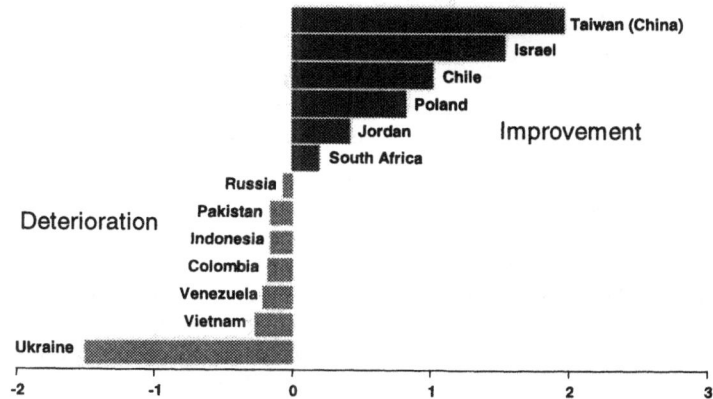

Source: Kaufmann, based on Global Competitiveness Survey

Box 6.1: Lessons from International Experience

In the nineteenth century, the United States and the United Kingdom successfully reformed their systems of public administration and procurement. Three aspects of the process of institutional reform account for its success. First, in both countries reform occurred under political systems that typically produced two balanced parties alternating in power, both of which shared in the benefits of reform. Second, reformist politicians in both countries successfully mobilized powerful business support for a more efficient public service. In the United States, urban reform was given a push when graft levels increased from 10 to 30 percent of the value of contracts. Businessmen were willing to tolerate a certain level of corruption, but began to protest when the level of graft escalated. Finally, the reforms became durable because they created a benevolent dynamic, in which partial changes created new allies, and evolved over time into full-scale reform.

Reform of the public service in the United States started slowly at the federal level and focused on parts of the bureaucracy in which new allies were produced by the process of change itself. Important constituencies outside government benefited and helped to institutionalize reform. Inside government, the first beneficiaries of civil service protection favored its preservation. Presidents about to leave office extended civil service protection to their appointees. The proportion covered by the merit system increased when overall government employment rose. Once the number of merit employees became large, they emerged as a potent interest group in favor of maintaining the system. The move from 10 to 80 percent civil service coverage took almost 40 years.

Despite its ultimate success, reform in the United States did not proceed in a straight line. In some cities, patronage-based and reformist administrations alternated in power. However, despite some backsliding, patronage-based systems often maintained the reforms introduced by progressive governments. Reforms were popular with the electorate and hard to reverse. Other countries have also begun their reform process with partial reforms. The customs service in Mexico, the reinsurance system in Argentina, and the city government of La Paz, have all recently experienced successful cleanups. Reform in Mexico was based on simplifying procedures and improving pay and monitoring. A scandal in Argentina led to changes in accounting practices. A reformist mayor in La Paz introduced a composite package of projects that began with efforts to remove the worst offenders but went on to include more fundamental changes.

Nevertheless, the durability of partial reforms is questionable. Reformers need to manage both the political and bureaucratic fallout of reform and find ways to enlist or out-maneuver potential opponents. In some cases, reform falters because of bad sequencing. Instead of generating a group of early winners who support continuing reform, the program may create early beneficiaries who fear that they will lose if reform continues. In the worst case they become a blocking coalition that prevents broad-based change.

Countries with different models of government have also been successful with anticorruption and governance reforms. The key elements in the already open economies of Hong Kong and Singapore were comprehensive and meritocratic public sector reforms, backed by fair and effective enforcement agencies. Both countries now have highly professional civil services, and Singapore's public service has rates of pay relative to the private sector that are among the highest in the world. Starting in 1974, Hong Kong took strong measures against corruption in the police force and the whole public service and launched an anticorruption strategy based on prevention, education, and enforcement. Over a 26-year period, they made dramatic reductions first in public sector corruption and, later on, in private sector corruption. Each year the Independent Commission Against Corruption surveys the population in order to study people's evolving perceptions and attitudes and refocus their preventive and educational efforts accordingly.

There are lessons here for reformers in the transition countries. Economic liberalization should proceed in tandem with efforts to establish transparency and accountability in state structures so that those who benefit from the emerging private sector cannot block subsequent efforts to improve the efficiency and fairness of the system. Equally critical to sustainable reforms are meritocratic, well-paid public administrations, backed by credible judicial and enforcement agencies and reinforced by good lines of communication with the population.

Based on Rose-Ackerman (1999, chapter 11) and sources cited within; and on advice from Bertrand de Speville (former Commissioner of the Hong Kong Independent Commission Against Corruption).

The challenge ahead for transition countries is to make a durable commitment to tackle corruption. The task will not be easy. The status quo often benefits powerful interests, making the political economy of anticorruption initiatives complex and difficult. Corruption has become pervasive in many transition countries. Capture has distorted the formal and informal rules of the game to encode the advantages of particular groups into the very framework of the new institutional environment. As the report has demonstrated, the roots of these problems reach deep into historical legacies, economic structures, and transition paths. Thus, while there may arise valuable windows of opportunity in specific countries, it remains important to manage expectations and underscore the long-term nature of reform.

But as the report has shown, reform and progress are possible and the costs of doing nothing are extremely high. Unbundling corruption and tailoring reform strategies to target the specific profile of the problem in different countries provide important insights into the design of effective anticorruption strategies. After ten years of transition, the building blocks of reform are now better known, but the challenge remains to prioritize and sequence these reforms in a manner that can build credible support for a sustainable process of change. By analyzing the factors underlying the *persistence* of corruption in different contexts, this report provides an approach for meeting this challenge. The World Bank, in partnership with domestic and international actors, stands ready to work with the countries in the region in implementing credible anticorruption strategies.

References

Adelman, Irma and Dusan Vujovic. 1997. "Institutional and Policy Aspects of Transition: An Empirical Analysis," Handbook on the Globalization of the World Economy, edited by Amnon Levy-Livermore, pp. 343-385, Northhampton, MA, USA: Edward Elgar Publishing, Inc., 1998.

Ades, Alberto and Rafael Di Tella. 1999. *Rents, Competition, and Corruption.* American Economic Review, 89 (4), pp. 982-993.

Anderson, James E. and Douglas Marcouiller. 1999. *Trade, Insecurity, and Home Bias: An Empirical Investigation.* NBER Working Paper 7000.

Anderson, James H. 1998. *Corruption in Latvia: Survey Evidence.* World Bank.

Anderson, James H. 2000. *Corruption in Slovakia: Results of Diagnostic Surveys.* World Bank.

Anderson, James H.; Omar Azfar; Daniel Kaufmann; Young Lee; Amitabha Mukherjee; and Randi Ryterman. 1999. *Corruption in Georgia: Survey Evidence.* World Bank draft.

Anderson, James H.; Jean-Jacques Dethier; Nora Dudwick; Kathleen Kuehnast; and Maria Shkaratan. 1999. *The Impact of Corruption on the Poor in Transition Countries.* World Bank draft.

Aslund, Anders. 1999. *Why has Russia's Economic Transformation Been So Arduous?* Annual World Bank Conference on Development Economics Paper: Paris, France.

Balcerowicz, Ewa; Leszek Balcerowicz; and Iraj Hashi, eds. 1999. *Barriers to Entry and Growth of Private Companies in Poland, the Czech Republic, Hungary, Albania and Lithuania.* CASE Reports, No. 14.

Blanchard, Olivier and Michael Kremer. 1997. *Disorganization.* Quarterly Journal of Economics, 112 (4).

Blocker, J. 1997. *Corruption among State Officials in Eastern Europe.* RFE-RL, 13 June.

Broadman, Harry G. and Francesca Recanatini. 2000. *Seeds of Corruption: Do Market Institutions Matter?* World Bank: Policy Research Working Paper No. 2368.

Campos, J. Edgardo; Donald Lien; and Sanjay Pradhan. 1999. *The Impact of Corruption on Investment: Predictability Matters.* World Development, Vol. 27, No. 6, pp. 1059-1067.

De Melo, Martha; Cevdet Denizer; Alan Gelb; and Stoyan Tenev. 1996. *From Plan to Market: Patterns of Transition.* World Bank: Policy Research Working Paper No. 1564.

De Melo, Martha; Cevdet Denizer; Alan Gelb; and Stoyan Tenev. 1997. "Circumstance and Choice: The Role of Initial Conditions and Policies in Transition Economies" World Bank Policy Research Working Paper 1866.

Desai, Raj M. and Itzhak Goldberg. 2000. *The Vicious Circles of Control: Regional Governments and Insiders in Privatized Russian Enterprises.* World Bank: Policy Research Working Paper No. 2287.

Dethier, Jean-Jacques. 1999a. *Governance and Economic Performance: A Survey.* ZEF Discussion Paper on Development Policy.

————. 1999b. *Governance and Poverty.* Quarterly Journal of International Agriculture, No. 4/99.

De Winter, Lieven. 2000. "Political Corruption in the Belgian Partitocracy: (Still) a Systemic Disease?" Robert Schuman Centre for Advanced Studies Working Paper No. 28.

Djankov, Simeon and Peter Murrell. 2000. *Enterprise Restructuring in Transition: A Quantitative Survey.* World Bank. Mimeo.

Dryzek, J. and Leslie J. Holmes, "The Real World of Civic Republicanism: Making Democracy Work in Poland and the Czech Republic" mimeo.

Dudwick, Nora. 1995. "Armenian Poverty Assessment Working Paper No. 1. A Qualitatitve assessment of the living standards of the Armenian population, October 1994-March 1995." The World Bank.

Easterly, William and Ross Levine. 1997. *Africa's Growth Tradegy[Tragedy?]: Policies and Ethnic Divisions.* Quarterly Journal of Economics, 112 (4), pp. 1203-1250.

Elkind, Peter. 2000. *The Incredible Half-Billion Dollar Azerbaijani Oil Swindle.* Fortune Magazine, 141 (5).

Elster, Jon; Claus Offe; and Ulrich K. Preuss; with Frank Boenker; Ulrike Goetting; and Friedbert W. Rueb. 1998. *Institutional Design in Post-communist Societies: Rebuilding the Ship at Sea.* Cambridge UK: Cambridge University Press.

European Bank for Reconstruction and Development (EBRD). 1999. *Transition Report. Chapter 6: Governance in Transition.* London: EBRD.

European Stability Initiative (ESI). 1999. *Reshaping International Priorities in Bosnia and Hercegovina.* October 14. Mimeo.

Financial Times. 2000. Apr 3rd.

Friedman, Eric; Simon Johnson; Daniel Kaufmann; and Pablo Zoido-Lobaton. 2000. *Dodging the Grabbing Hand: The Determinants of Unofficial Activity in 69 Countries.* Journal of Public Economics, 76, pp. 459-493.

Galligan, Denis J. and Daniel M. Smilov, eds. 1999 *Administrative law in Central and Eastern Europe, 1996-1998*. Budapest ; New York : Central European University Press ; Ithaca, N.Y. : Distributed in the U.S. by Cornell University Press Services.

Gupta, Sanjeev; Hamid Davoodi; and Rosa Alonso-Terme. 1998. *Does Corruption Affect Income Inequality and Poverty?* IMF Working Paper.

Hellman, Joel. 1998. *Winners Take All: The Politics of Partial Reform in Post Communist Transition*. World Politics, 50 (2), pp.203-234.

Hellman, Joel; Geraint Jones; and Daniel Kaufmann. 2000a. *Seize the State, Seize the Day: An Empirical Analysis of State Capture and Corruption in Transition*. World Bank. Mimeo. Presented at the Annual Bank Conference in Development Economics, April 18-20, 2000, Washington, DC.

————. 2000b. "Are Foreign Investors and Multinationals Engaging in Corrupt Practices in Transition Economies?" Transition, Vol. 11 No 3-4, May-June-July 2000, pp. 4-7.

Hellman, Joel; Geraint Jones; Daniel Kaufmann; and Mark Schankerman. 2000. *Measuring Governance, Corruption and State Capture: How Firms and Bureaucrats Shape the Business Environment*. World Bank: Policy Research Paper No. 2312.

Heybey, Berta and Peter Murrell. 1999. *The Relationship between Economic Growth and the Speed of Liberalization During Transition*. Journal of Policy Reform, 3(2), pp. 121-137.

Holmes, Leslie. Forthcoming. "Crime, Corruption and Politics: International and Transnational Factors" in A. Pravda and J. Zielonka (eds.), *Democratic Consolidation in Eastern Europe: International and Transnational Factors* (provisionally Oxford University Press, forthcoming), 27 pp. in ms.

Holmes, Leslie. 2000. *High Level Political Corruption in CEE and CIS, and its Implications for Reform Efforts and System Consolidation.* Mimeo. World Bank.

Holmes, Leslie. 1999. "Corruption in Europe," *Dialogue*, Vol.18, No.2, pp.19-25.

Holmes, Leslie and Wojciech Roszkowski, eds. 1997. *Changing Rules: Polish Political and Economic Transformation in Comparative Perspective*. Warsaw.

Holovaty, Sergyi. 2000. *Background Report on Corruption in Ukraine*. Mimeo. World Bank.

Johnson, Simon; Daniel Kaufmann; and Andrei Shleifer. 1997. *The Unofficial Economy in Transition*. Brookings Papers on Economic Activity, 2, pp. 159-239.

Johnson, Simon; Daniel Kaufmann; and Pablo Zoido-Lobaton. 1998a. *Corruption, Public Finances and the Unofficial Economy*. Mimeo.

————. 1998b. *Regulatory Discretion and the Unofficial Economy.* Presented at the 110th Annual Meeting of the American Economic Association, January 3-5, 1998.

Johnson, Simon; Daniel Kaufmann; John McMillan; and Christopher Woodruff. 2000. *Why Do Firms Hide? Bribes and Unofficial Activity after Communism.* Journal of Public Economics, 76, pp. 495-520.

Kaid, Linda Lee and Holtz-Bacha, Christina (1995). "Political Advertising in Western Democracies: Parties and Candidates on Television," Sage Publications 1995.

Karatnycky, Adrian; Alexander Motyl; and Charles Graybow, eds. 1998. *Nations in Transit.* New Jersey: Freedom House.

Kaufmann, Daniel. 1997. *Corruption: The Facts.* Foreign Policy, Summer 1997, pp. 114-130.

Kaufmann, Daniel and Paul Seigelbaum. 1996. *Privatization and Corruption in Transition Economies.* Journal of International Affairs, 50, No. 2, pp 419-458.

Kaufmann, Daniel and Shang-Jin Wei. 1999. *Does "Grease Money" Speed Up the Wheels of Commerce?* National Bureau of Economic Research, Working Paper 7093. Cambridge, MA: Harvard University.

Kaufmann, Daniel; Aart Kraay; and Pablo Zoido-Lobaton. 1999a. *Aggregating Governance Indicators.* World Bank: Policy Research Paper No. 2195.

————. 1999b. *Governance Matters.* World Bank: Policy Research Paper No. 2196.

Kaufmann, Daniel; Sanjay Pradhan; and Randi S. Ryterman. 1998. *New Frontiers in Diagnosing and Combating Corruption.* World Bank: PREM Note No. 7.

Kaufmann, Daniel; Auron Pasha; Zef Preci; Randi Ryterman; and Pablo Zoido-Lobaton. 1998. *Governance and Corruption in Albania: The Imperative of Institutional Reforms.* ACER/World Bank draft.

King, Anthony 2000. "Principles of Political Party Financing," Paper for the conference of the Speaker of the Polish Parliament on *Corruption in Politics,* Parliament, Warsaw, April 26, 2000

Klitgaard, Robert E. 1988. *Controlling Corruption.* Berkeley: University of California Press.

Knack, Stephen and Gary Anderson. 1999. *Is "Good Governance" Progressive? Institutions, Inequality, and Poverty Reduction.* Presented at the 1999 Annual Meeting of the American Political Science Association, Atlanta.

Laffont, Jean-Jacques and Jean Tirole. 1993. *A Theory of Incentives in Procurement and Regulation.* Cambridge, MA: MIT Press.

La Porta, Raphael; F. Lopez-de-Silanes; A. Shleifer; and R.W. Vishny. 1997. *Legal Determinants of External Finance.* Journal of Finance, 52 (3), pp. 1131-1150.

La Porta, Raphael; F. Lopez-de-Silanes; A. Shleifer; and R.W. Vishny. 1999. *The Quality of Government.* Journal of Economics, Law and Organization, 15 (1), pp. 222-279.

Lieberman, Ira W. and Rogi Veimetra. 1996. *The Rush for State Shares in the "Klondyke" of Wild West Capitalism: Loans-for-Shares Transactions in Russia.* The George Washington Journal of International Law and Economics, 29 (3), pp. 737-768.

Lewis, Maureen. 1999. *Informal Health Payments in Eastern Europe and Central Asia: Issues, Trends and Policy Implications.* Paper prepared for the Health Observatory Meeting, Venice, Italy, December 3-4, 1999.

Mauro, Paulo. 1995. *Corruption and Growth.* Quarterly Journal of Economics, 110 (3), pp. 681-712.

Mauro, Paolo. 1997. *The Effects of Corruption on Growth, Investment, and Government Expenditure: A Cross-Country Analysis*, in Kimberly Ann Elliot, ed., 1997, *Corruption and the Global Economy*, Washington, DC: Institute for International Economics.

Mauro, Paolo. 1998. *Corruption and the Composition of Government Expenditure.* Journal of Public Economics, 69, pp. 263-279.

McCormack, Gillian, ed. 1999. *Media in the CIS: A Study of the Political, Legislative and Socio-Economic Framework.* Düsseldorf: The European Institute for the Media.

Mirzoev, Tokhir. 1999. *Corruption in Tajikistan as Seen by the Private Sector.* Dushanbe, Tajikstan. September. Mimeo.

Murrell, Peter; Karen Turner Dunn; and Georges Korsun. 1996. *The Culture of Policy-Making in the Transition from Socialism: Price Policy in Mongolia.* Economic Development and Cultural Change, 45(1), pp.175-194.

Murrell, Peter. 1992. *Evolution in Economics and in the Economic Reform of the Centrally Planned Economies. In* Christopher C. Clague and Gordon Rausser, eds., *The Emergence of Market Economies in Eastern Europe.* Cambridge, MA: Blackwell.

Narayan, Deepa; Raj Patel; Kai Schafft; Anne Rademacher; Sarah Koch-Schulte; Robert Chambers; Meera Shah; and Patti Petesch. 2000. *Voices of the Poor.* World Bank.

Nelson, Mark; Vitaliy Kartamychev; Irina Borisovna Garsia; Fiona Harrison; and Vladimir Svetozarov. 1999. *Anticorruption in Transition: The Role of the Media.* World Bank. Mimeo.

Olson, Mancur. 1965. *The Logic of Collective Action.* Cambridge, MA: Harvard University Press.

Paul, Samuel. 1999. *Civil Society Interventions Against Corruption: A Review of Projects from the Eastern and Central European Countries.* World Bank. Mimeo.

Philp, Mark. 2000a. *Access, Accountability and Authority: Corruption and the Democratic Process.*, Oxford, UK, February. Unpublished.

Philp, Mark. 2000b. *Corruption Control and the Transfer of Regulatory Frameworks.* Paper prepared for the World Bank Workshop on Anticorruption for academics and practitioners, Warsaw, May 19. Mimeo.

Pujas, Veronique and Rhodes, Martin (1999) : "Party Finance and Political Scandal in Italy, Spain and France" Western European Politics, Vol 22, No. 3 (July 1999) pp 41-63.

Recanatini, Francesca and Randi Ryterman. 2000. *Disorganization or Self-Organization.* World Bank. Mimeo.

Rhodes, Martin. 1997. "Party Finance in Italy: A Case of Systemic Corruption," West European Politics, 20, 1, pp. 54-80. (Also in M. Bull and M. Rhodes (eds.), Crisis and Transition in Italian Politics, London: Frank Cass 1997, pp. 54-80.)

Rose-Ackerman, Susan. 1999. *Corruption and Government: Causes, Consequences and Reform.* Cambridge UK: Cambridge University Press.

Rosenburg, Tina. 1995. *The Haunted Land: Facing Europe's Ghosts After Communism.* New York: Random House, Inc.

Schneider, Friedrich and Dominik Enste. 1998. *Increasing Shadow Economies All Over the World—Fiction or Reality (A Survey of the Global Evidence of its Size and of its Impact from 1970 to 1995).* August 21, 1998. Draft.

Scott, James C. 1972. *Comparative Political Corruption.* New Jersey: Prentice Hall.

Sutch, Helen; Jacek Wojciechowicz; and Michal Dybula. 2000. *Corruption in Poland: Review of Priority Areas and Proposals for Action.* World Bank. March.

Svensson, Jakob. 1998. *Foreign Aid and Rent-Seeking.* World Bank. February. Mimeo (forthcoming in the Journal of International Economics).

Tanzi, Vito. 1998. *Corruption Around the World: Causes, Consequences, Scope and Cures.* IMF Working Paper.

Tanzi, Vito and Hamid Davoodi. 1997. *Corruption, Public Investment and Growth.* IMF Working Paper 97/139.

Transnational Center for Crime and Corruption (TraCCC). 2000. *Half Way Home and a Long Way to Go: Challenges of Corruption and Reform Implementation Facing the Post-Soviet States.* Mimeo.

Treisman, Daniel. 2000. *The Causes of Corruption: A Cross-National Study.* Journal of Public Economics ,76, pp. 399-457.

Wanner, Catherine and Nora Dudwick. 1996. *Ethnographic Study of Poverty in Ukraine.* World Bank.

Wedel, Janine R. 2000. *Toward an Anti-Corruption Agenda for the Soviet Development Team.* Mimeo.

Wei, Shang-Jin. 1999a. *How Taxing is Corruption on International Investors?* The Review of Economics and Statistics, Vol. 81, No. 4, pp. 1-12.

————. 1999b. *Corruption in Economic Development: Beneficial Grease, Minor Annoyance or Major Obstacle.* World Bank: Policy Research Working Paper No. 2048.

Wei, Shang-Jin. 2000. *Bribery in the Economies: Grease or Sand?* Harvard University, NBER, and the World Bank. February 3. Mimeo.

Wei, Shang-Jin and Sara Sievers. 1999. "The Cost of Crony Capitalism," in *The Asian Competitiveness Report 1999.* Geneva: World Economic Forum, pp. 50-55.

World Bank. 1993. *World Development Report.* World Bank, Washington DC.

World Bank. 1997. *World Development Report: The State in a Changing World.* Oxford University Press.

World Bank. 1999. *World Development Indicators.* World Bank, Washington DC.

World Bank. 2000. *Making the Transition Work for Everyone: Poverty and Inequality in Europe and Central Asia.* World Bank. April 2000. Draft.

World Bank. 2000. The Road to Stability and Prosperity in South Eastern Europe – A Regional Strategy Paper. Washington, DC.

Zak, Paul J. and Steven Knack. 1998. *Trust and Growth.* SSRN Working Paper.

Zvekiv, Ugljesa. 1998. *Criminal Victimisation in Countries in Transition.* United Nations Interregional Crime and Justice Research Institute, Publication No. 61. Rome.

Annex 1. Methodological Notes for Figures in the Text

The purpose of this Annex is to provide greater detail on the sources, statistical significance, and methodological issues associated with the Figures presented in the text.

Chapter 1. The Level and Pattern of Corruption in Transition Countries

Figure 1.1: **World-wide Perceptions of Corruption**

Figure 1.1 presents a worldwide comparison of corruption based on an aggregate index (Kaufmann, Kraay, and Zoido-Lobaton 1999a). The authors construct the aggregate index for each country on the basis of the 12 most widely available corruption indices. Error bars are provided to give a rough indication of the statistical margin of error associated with each region's estimate. The estimation of these margins of error is based on the margins of error of each country in the regional groupings. However, the component indices themselves are estimates with (unknown) margins of errors, suggesting that simple standard errors of regional averages may be understated. In an attempt to mitigate this bias, the error bars in Figure 1.1 are calculated on the conservative assumption that the errors are perfectly correlated, which tends to bias the error estimates in the opposite direction.

Figure 1.2: **Administrative Corruption (bribes as a share of annual revenues)**

This measure of administrative corruption is based on a survey question about the amount of bribes paid by enterprises as a share of annual revenues. Since it is based on a survey (the BEEPS), the margin of error of the estimates can be explicitly calculated, and error bars (representing ± one standard deviation) are included in the figure. The measure of administrative corruption in Figure 1.2 differs from the "bribe tax" presented in EBRD (1999), although both were based on the BEEPS. The measure used in this report includes the responses of *all* firms, whereas the measure presented in EBRD (1999) presents the average bribes as a share of revenues, among firms that reported paying bribes.

Figure 1.3: **State Capture Index**

This measure of state capture was developed by Hellman, Jones, and Kaufmann (2000a). The calculation of the margin of error for the state capture index is more complex than that of administrative corruption, since it is the average of six subindices, each with their own associated statistical error. To calculate the standard error of the overall index an assumption must be made about the correlation between the measurement errors of the components. The standard error of the aggregate index of state capture is calculated on the conservative assumption that the errors of the components are perfectly correlated. The estimated standard error of the index of state capture should therefore be interpreted as an upper bound to the true standard error.

A further issue concerns the definition of state capture. The measure presented in the report comprises six components—"sale" of (i) parliamentary votes and (ii) presidential decrees to private interests; the sale of (iii) civil and (iv) criminal court decisions to private interests; (v) corrupt mishandling of central bank funds; and (vi) illegal contributions by private actors to political parties. Table A.1, below, presents alternative estimates of state capture, excluding court decisions and mishandling of central bank funds, whose link to the concept of state capture is relatively more tenuous than the purchase of legislation and politics. (See endnote 16 to Chapter 1.) The alternative measures of state capture are very similar to the one use used in the report. Table A.2 provides the correlation coefficients between the alternative measures of state capture. In all cases, the correlation exceeds 0.97. Finally, it should be noted that since the standard errors of the components of the index of state capture were assumed to be perfectly correlated, a very conservative assumption, an index with fewer components would not be less precise than the index used in this report.

Table A.1 The Effect of Excluding Central Bank and Courts from the Measurement of State Capture

Country	State Capture including all components	State Capture excluding central bank	State Capture excluding courts	State Capture excluding both central bank and courts
Albania	16	13	17	15
Armenia	7	8	7	8
Azerbaijan	41	41	40	38
Bulgaria	28	31	29	33
Croatia	27	26	27	26
Czech Rep.	11	12	11	12
Estonia	10	12	11	13
Georgia	24	27	24	27
Hungary	7	8	7	8
Kazakhstan	12	12	13	13
Kyrgyz Rep.	29	30	32	35
Latvia	30	33	26	28
Lithuania	12	11	12	12
Moldova	37	39	38	42
Poland	12	10	12	10
Romania	21	24	21	25
Russia	32	35	31	35
Slovak Rep.	24	22	26	26
Slovenia	7	7	7	8
Ukraine	32	37	31	37

**Table A.2 Correlation Coefficient for
Alternative Measures of Capture**

	State Capture including all components	State Capture excluding central bank	State Capture excluding courts	State Capture excluding both central bank and courts
State Capture including all components	1.000			
State Capture excluding central bank	0.986	1.000		
State Capture excluding courts	0.992	0.971	1.000	
State Capture excluding both central bank and courts	0.975	0.983	0.983	1.000

Figure 1.4:   Typology of Corruption

Based on Figures 1.2 and 1.3 a typology of corruption in the transition economies is developed, generating the scatter plot in Figure 1.4. For the purposes of analysis in subsequent chapters, the countries in Figure 1.4 have been divided into four groups on the basis of thresholds of administrative corruption and state capture. This produces a two-by-two matrix that groups countries on the basis of similarities in both the level and pattern of corruption.

Figure 1.4 has been reproduced in Figure A.1, below, with dotted lines added to distinguish between the four groups of countries. The composition of the groups is based on the determination of these dividing lines, which is done here for analytical purposes only. As several countries lay close to the thresholds, their inclusion into either group is subject to a greater margin of error. However, the availability of estimates of standard errors makes it possible to estimate the probability that a country has been misclassified, even within the empirical typology presented in the Report. (As stressed in the text, the typology is "not intended to define absolute and unambiguous divisions among countries. Rather it is presented as a heuristic device to highlight analytically and empirically the differences in patterns of corruption across countries.")

92

Figure A.1. Typology of Corruption, with Risk of Misclassification

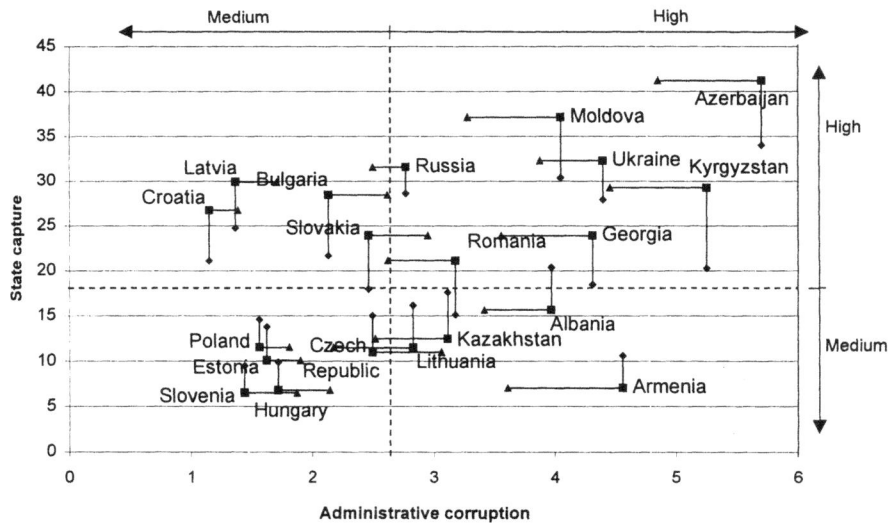

Source: BEEPS

Figure A.1 illustrates the typology with point estimates (depicted by the symbol ■) as well as estimates of 90 percent limit values in the direction of the other quadrants. For the medium/medium quadrant, for example: one could be 90 percent certain that the true value of state capture lies below the point ♦, and 90 percent certain that the true value of administrative corruption lies to the left of the point ▲. This is equivalent to carrying out a one-tailed test of the difference between the point estimate for each country and the (arbitrary) dividing line. For those countries for which ♦ or ▲ lie in a different quadrant from ■, there is less than 90 percent chance that the country is correctly classified in that particular dimension. The method of calculating the confidence intervals assumes, for the sake of simplicity, that the position of the dividing lines is independent of the uncertainty in the point estimates.

The one-tailed tests described above were also used to estimate the probability of misclassification, and the estimates are presented in Table A.3, below. On the dimension of state capture, only three countries – Albania, Slovakia and Romania – demonstrate a reasonable risk of misclassification. The measure of administrative corruption has a more continuous distribution with more countries having a non-negligible risk of misclassification, including the Czech Republic, Kazakhstan, Lithuania, Romania, Slovakia and Russia.

Country	Table A.3 – One-tailed tests for misclassification Probability of misclassification with a one-tailed test Administrative corruption	State capture
Albania	0.00	0.23
Armenia	0.00	0.00
Azerbaijan	0.00	0.00
Bulgaria	0.09	0.03
Croatia	0.00	0.03
Czech Rep.	**0.38**	0.01
Estonia	0.00	0.00
Georgia	0.00	0.10
Hungary	0.00	0.00
Kazakhstan	**0.15**	0.07
Kyrgyz Rep.	0.00	0.06
Latvia	0.00	0.00
Lithuania	**0.35**	0.03
Moldova	0.01	0.00
Poland	0.00	0.00
Romania	**0.10**	**0.28**
Russia	**0.26**	0.00
Slovak Rep.	**0.33**	**0.12**
Slovenia	0.00	0.00
Ukraine	0.00	0.00

Countries with a greater than 10% chance of misclassification are highlighted in bold

The discussion above centers on statistical margin of error. A second potential source of error could arise if the quality of the survey implementation varied greatly across countries, or if there are systematic differences in respondents' perceptions of the severity of otherwise identical problems in different countries. However, the BEEPS was carried out by the same international company in all countries except two (Latvia and Albania) to ensure consistency, so variation in the quality of survey implementation is not a concern. Furthermore Hellman, Jones, Kaufmann, and Schankerman (2000) test for the presence of systematic cross-country biases in the BEEPS (whatever their source) using a methodology that compares estimates derived from the BEEPS with measures of the same concept from other sources. They find no evidence of such bias.

Figure A.2 State Capture and Captor Firms

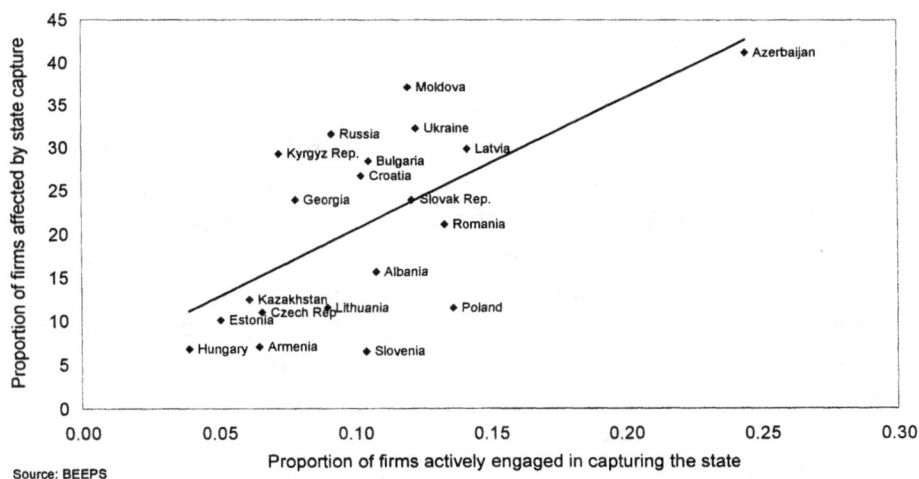

Source: BEEPS

The measure of state capture used throughout this report represents the proportion of firms that report being affected by state capture, whether or not the firms actively engage in state capture. The reason is that the degree to which a state is captured is not necessarily related to the number of firms that engage in such forms of influence, but the extent to which the formation of policy is distorted by private interests.

The levels of state capture and the proportion of firms that engage in capture are positively related. Figure A.2 presents a scatterplot demonstrating the high correlation (correlation coefficient = 0.69) between the index of the perception of state capture and active engagement in such activity. Even after removing Azerbaijan, which appears to be an outlier, the correlation remains high: the correlation coefficient becomes 0.51 and the slope coefficient is significant at the 5 percent level. These correlations give some additional confidence in the state capture index used throughout this report.

Chapter 2. The Economic and Social Consequences of Corruption in Transition Economies

All of the figures in Chapter 2 show the average of some variable over the countries in each of the four typologies, as depicted in Figure 1.4. The theme of Chapter 2, the economic and social consequences of corruption, calls for analysis whereby corruption is the *cause* of certain social ills.

Empirical analyses of causation are inherently difficult, and the timing and availability of data exacerbate the difficulty. First, as discussed in the text, there may be multiple feedback loops between corruption as a cause and a consequence of various economic and social problems, and both are further influenced by yet other factors. Given a static data set with only 20 observations, there are clear limits to the degree of sophistication one can expect from any model. Second, the BEEPS was undertaken in the summer of 1999, in many cases *after* the measurement of what we would normally think of as the dependent variables. Given this timing, establishing causation would be difficult indeed. Similarly, controlling for factors that may be influencing levels of all three variables of interest—administrative corruption, state capture, and whichever "cost" is being investigated—faces similar hurdles of complex interactions and a small number of cross-country observations.

The charts in Chapter 2, therefore, do not attempt to control for other factors or to establish empirically a direction of causation. Rather, they depict the simple association between the variable of interest and levels of administrative corruption and state capture. Their purpose is not to provide empirical evidence of causation, but to show that the data are consistent with the idea, reasoned in the text, that corruption is deleterious for society, even if the figures themselves only depict simple correlations between variables. While the figures in Chapter 2 make no attempt to control for external factors or to establish causation, the broader literature on governance and corruption, availing itself of a greater number of countries and governance indicators, includes studies that support the ideas argued in the text—that corruption does indeed pose quantitatively large economic and social consequences on society.

Table A.4 presents simple evidence that the figures in Chapter 2 represent relationships that are statistically significant, even if not so in a *ceteris paribus* sense.

Table A.4 Statistical Relationships between Chapter 2 "Consequences" and State Capture and Administrative Corruption

| Figure and Variable of Interest | Simple t-test between High-High and the Medium-Medium groups of countries | OLS Regressions | | | | |
| | | t-statistics of coefficients (p-value in parentheses) | | | | |
		Administrative Corruption	State Capture	F (p-value)	N	R-sq
2.1 Output decline	5.33 (0.00)	2.02* (0.06)	2.84** (0.02)	0.01	20	0.55
2.2 Poverty	2.81 (0.01)	3.88*** (0.00)	0.04 (0.97)	0.00	19	0.54
2.3 Gini coefficient	3.03 (0.01)	2.29** (0.04)	0.81 (0.43)	0.06	17	0.34
2.4 Unofficial economy	3.17 (0.01)	2.04* (0.07)	1.35 (0.20)	0.01	15	0.56
2.5 Macro governance	4.24 (0.00)	1.81* (0.09)	1.28 (0.22)	0.03	20	0.27
2.6 Organized crime	4.57 (0.00)	1.93* (0.02)	1.78* (0.02)	0.01	20	0.42
One-tailed tests, assuming equal variances. (p-values in parentheses)		Significance levels: * = 10 percent level; ** = 5 percent level; *** = 1 percent level.				

Figure 2.1:   Corruption and Output Decline

Output decline is the percentage decline in GDP between 1989 and 1998. All countries in Figure 1.4 are included in Figure 2.1. The data are based on Table 3.1.1 of EBRD *Transition Report 1999*, p. 73. See Table A.4 for an indication of simple statistical significance.

Hellman, Jones, and Kaufmann (2000a) use the BEEPS data to examine (with controlled regressions) the impact of corruption on investment at the firm level. Additional empirical studies on the relationship between corruption and growth and investment include: Mauro (1995, 1997), Kaufmann (1997), World Bank (1997), Tanzi (1998), Kaufmann and Wei (1999), Campos, Lien, and Pradhan (1999), and Wei (1999a, 1999b, and 2000).

Figure 2.2:   Corruption and Poverty

Poverty is represented by the percentage of the population living on less than $2.15 per day. (See Table A.4 for an indication of simple statistical significance.) All countries in Figure 1.4 are included in Figure 2.2, with the exception of the Slovak Republic. The data are drawn from the World Bank report, also prepared for the 2000 Annual Meetings in Prague, *Making the Transition Work for Everyone: Poverty and Inequality in Europe and Central Asia*, Chapter 1, Table 1. This "poverty head-count" is based on household surveys undertaken in 1996-1999 (surveys from 1998 or 1999 were used for most countries; Bulgaria's headcount is based on a 1995 survey). Income levels of have been PPP adjusted.

Additional empirical studies on the relationship between corruption and poverty include Knack and Anderson (1999), and Gupta, Davoodi, and Alonso-Terme (1998). Kaufmann, Kraay, and Zoido-Lobaton (1999b) show the relationship between poor governance and nonpecuniary measures of well-being such as infant mortality. See also, World Bank (2000) *Making the Transition Work for Everyone: Poverty and Inequality in Europe and Central Asia.*

Figure 2.3:   Corruption and Income Inequality
Income inequality is represented by the Gini coefficient and is drawn from the World Bank report, also prepared for the 2000 Annual Meetings in Prague, *Making the Transition Work for Everyone: Poverty and Inequality in Europe and Central Asia*, Chapter 4, Table 1. The Gini coefficients are World Bank estimates based on household surveys from 1996-1999. All countries in Figure 1.4 are included in Figure 2.4, except Azerbaijan, the Slovak Republic, and Ukraine. See Table A.4 for an indication of simple statistical significance.

The relationship between corruption and inequality has also been examined in Gupta, Davoodi, and Alonso-Terme (1998), and Knack and Anderson (1999). See also, World Bank (2000) *Making the Transition Work for Everyone: Poverty and Inequality in Europe and Central Asia.*

Figure 2.4:   The Unofficial Economy
Estimates of the unofficial economy, based on changes in electric power consumption and officially measured GDP, are drawn from Johnson, Kaufmann, and Shleifer (1997). All countries in Figure 1.4 are included in Figure 2.5, except Albania, Armenia, Croatia, the Kyrgyz Republic, and Slovenia. See Table A.4 for an indication of simple statistical significance.

Studies of the unofficial economy and its link to corruption include Johnson, Kaufmann, and Shleifer (1997), Johnson, Kaufmann, and Zoido-Lobaton (1998), Johnson, Kaufmann, McMillan, and Woodruff (2000), and Friedman, Johnson, Kaufmann, and Zoido-Lobaton (2000). See also Kaufmann, Pradhan, and Ryterman (1998) for an illustration of the degree to which corruption leads to a loss in tax revenues.

Figure 2.5:   Quality of Macroeconomic Governance
Macroeconomic governance is an index measuring the extent to which policy instability, exchange rate instability, and inflation are obstacles for business. The data are drawn from the BEEPS. An almost identical index is presented in Table 6.1 of EBRD *Transition Report 1999*, p. 116. All countries in Figure 1.4 are included in Figure 2.6. See Table A.4 for an indication of simple statistical significance.

The relationship between corruption and budget distortions has been examined in Mauro (1998), and the effect on international trade in Anderson and Marcouiller (1999).

Figure 2.6: Organized Crime as a Problem Doing Business
Organized crime is the percentage of firms that reported that organized crime is a problem doing business in the BEEPS. All countries in Figure 1.4 are included in Figure 2.7. See Table A.4 for an indication of simple statistical significance.

Chapter 3. The Origins of Corruption in Transition Countries

The challenges of analyzing the costs of corruption—paucity of cross-country observations and mis-timed data—are not so formidable for analyses of the origins of corruption. (i) Influences on firm-level decisions regarding corruption can be unearthed using firm-level analysis, for which the BEEPS provides thousands of observations. (ii) Since the object of investigation is the set of *causes* of state capture and administrative corruption, the fact that both are measured in 1999 is entirely consistent with such a model. For these reasons, the analysis of the origins of corruption in transition countries was able to benefit from a multivariate framework. While still stopping short of addressing all possible endogeneity issues, this approach does provide a measure of rigor beyond what was possible in Chapter 2.

Underpinning this analysis in Chapter 3 are a series of firm-level regressions, in which state capture and administrative corruption are explained by firm, industry, and country characteristics. These characteristics include: (i) the size, ownership form, and age of the firm; (ii) dummy variables describing the industry of the firm and its membership in a business association; and (iii) variables measuring institutional legacies of a country, such as the natural log of the number of years it was a state in the last century, a dummy variable indicating whether it was a member of the CIS, a dummy variable indicating whether it had been part of the Habsburg Monarchy, a dummy variable indicating whether it was centrally planned (as opposed to labor managed or market socialist), an index of political liberalization at the onset of transition, an index of economic liberalization at the onset of transition, a dummy variable indicating whether it was resource rich, and more. Generally, those variables described by the figures in the text were those that were significant and robust to many different specifications. Surprisingly, a dummy variable measuring whether a country is in the CIS was useful in explaining administrative corruption, but not state capture.

98

Table A.5 Statistical Relationships between Chapter 3 "Origins" and State Capture and Administrative Corruption

| Figure and Variable of Interest | Simple t-test between High-High and the Medium-Medium groups of countries | OLS Regressions | | N | R-sq |
| | | t-statistics of coefficients of variable of interest (p-value in parentheses) | | | |
		Administrative Corruption regressed on variable of interest	State Capture regressed on variable of interest		
3.1 Statehood (log)	1.51* (0.08)	-1.89* (0.07)		20	0.17
			-1.30 (0.21)	20	0.09
3.2 Habsburg legacy	4.83*** (0.00)	-3.06*** (0.01)		20	0.34
			-1.85* (0.08)	20	0.16
3.3 Democracy	5.51*** (0.00)	-4.06*** (0.00)		20	0.48
			-2.27** (0.04)	20	0.22
3.4 Resource endowments	0.87 (0.20)	1.12 (0.28)		20	0.07
			1.18 (0.25)	20	0.07
3.5 Change in leadership	3.23*** (0.01)	-1.13 (0.27)		20	0.07
			-2.81** (0.02)	20	0.30
One-tailed tests, assuming equal variances. (p-values in parentheses)		Significance levels: * = 10 percent level; ** = 5 percent level; *** = 1 percent level.			

Figure 3.1: Statehood and Corruption

The measure of experience with sovereignty is the number of years during the previous century that the country was a sovereign state. Of course, during this period, national borders for countries shifted dramatically. For the purposes of this analysis, a country continues to be classified as a sovereign nation following a significant change in its borders as long as the central government continues to be administered from its capital city. Thus, Russia and the Czech Republic are classified as sovereign nations during their Soviet and Czechoslovak periods, respectively, while the other states in the former Soviet Union and the Slovak Republic are not. All countries in Figure 1.4 are included in Figure 3.1. See Table A.5 for an indication of simple statistical significance.

Figure 3.2: Habsburg Legacy and Corruption

The countries that were formerly part of the Habsburg monarchy are Croatia, the Czech Republic, Hungary, Poland, the Slovak Republic, and Slovenia. All countries in Figure 1.4 are included in Figure 3.2. See Table A.5 for an indication of simple statistical significance.

Figure 3.3:   Democracy and Corruption
The data on democracy comes from Adelman and Vujovic (1997). The measure of democracy is an average of measures of the political independence of the country, the existence of a multiparty system, presence of political opposition, degree of political decentralization, role of elections in the political system, freedom of speech, and freedom to organize. All countries in Figure 1.4 are included in Figure 3.3. See Table A.5 for an indication of simple statistical significance.

Figure 3.4:   Resource Endowments and Corruption
The countries that are resource-rich, for the purposes of Figure 3.4, are Azerbaijan, Romania, Russia, and Kazakhstan. All countries in Figure 1.4 are included in Figure 3.4. Although Table A.5 suggests that resource endowments are only weakly related to administrative corruption and state capture, in a multivariate framework, resource endowments are consistently significant. See Table A.5 for an indication of simple statistical significance.

Figure 3.5:   Change in Leadership and Corruption
The countries with early changes in leadership are Armenia, Czech Republic, Estonia, Georgia, Hungary, Kyrgyz Republic, Latvia, Lithuania, Poland, the Slovak Republic, and Slovenia. All countries in Figure 1.4 are included in Figure 3.5. See Table A.5 for an indication of simple statistical significance.

Figure 3.6:   Economic and Political Reform and State Capture
The degree of economic reforms was measure by the EBRD Transition Indicators, 1999. The level of civil liberties is the three year average of the Freedom House Civil Liberties Index, which is based on assessments of freedom of expression and belief, association and organizational rights, rule of law and human rights, personal autonomy and economic rights. Figure 3.6 plots regression fits based on a regression of state capture (SC) on civil liberties (CL) and economic reforms (ER). A quadratic term is included for civil liberties to allow for curvature in the relationship. Basic regression statistics are presented below. (A constant was included but is not reported; t-statistics are in parentheses.) The regression was presented in Hellman, Jones, and Kaufmann (2000a), which also contains a broader discussion of the relationship between political and economic liberalization and state capture.

$$SC = a + \underset{(1.93)^*}{0.359} \; CL - \underset{(1.97)^*}{0.056} \; CL^2 - \underset{(1.87)^*}{0.143} \; ER \qquad R\text{-sq} = 0.513$$

Figure 3.7:   Foreign Direct Investment and Corruption
Data in Figure 3.7 are based on the BEEPS and draw on Hellman, Jones, and Kaufmann (2000b). Firms were grouped into three categories: (i) those with no foreign direct investment (FDI), (ii) those that have FDI and whose headquarters was domestically located, and (iii) those that have FDI and whose headquarters are located in another country. Pairwise t-tests of the levels of administrative corruption and state capture for these sets of countries are presented Table A.6, below.

Table A.6 Significance of FDI (and Location of Headquarters) for Levels of Administrative Corruption and State Capture

| | Pairwise t-tests for Differences in Means | | |
Variable 1	Variable 2	Administrative Corruption	State Capture
Firms with no FDI	Firms with FDI and Domestic HQ	0.16 (0.43)	2.58*** (0.01)
Firms with no FDI	Firms with FDI and Foreign HQ	2.28** (0.02)	1.60* (0.06)
Firms with FDI and Domestic HQ	Firms with FDI and Foreign HQ	2.47*** (0.01)	2.44*** (0.01)
One-tailed tests, assuming equal variances. (p-values in parentheses)		Significance levels: * = 10 percent level; ** = 5 percent level; *** = 1 percent level.	

Figure 3.8:   Foreign Direct Investment in High-Corruption Countries

Data in Figure 3.8 are based on the BEEPS and draw on Hellman, Jones, and Kaufmann (2000b).   Firms are divided into three groups as described above for Figure 3.7.   Figure 3.8 then shows the average percent of firms that engage in capture and the percentage of firm revenue paid in bribes, across firms in high and medium capture countries, respectively.   For both of the charts in Figure 3.8, active capture and administrative corruption are most prevalent among firms with FDI and domestic headquarters, *but only in high capture countries*.

Figure 3.9: Variation Within and Between Sub-regions

The data for Figure 3.9 are drawn from the BEEPS. Figure 3.9 simply presents the levels of administrative corruption and state capture for each country, according to the indicated sub-regions.

Chapter 4. A Multi-pronged Strategy for Combating Corruption

Chapter 4 has only two charts that suggest statistical relationships. Simple statistics on the significance of the relationships are presented in Table A.6. As discussed earlier, these relationships are not *ceteris paribus* but are merely presented as illustrations of a statistical association.

Table A.6 Statistical Relationships of Chapter 4 Charts

| | | OLS Regressions | | | | |
| Figure and Variable of Interest | Simple t-test between High-High and the Medium-Medium groups of countries | t-statistics of coefficients (p-value in parentheses) | | | | |
		Administrative Corruption	State Capture	F (p-value)	N	R-sq
4.2 Media repression	7.50 (0.00)	3.02*** (0.01)	1.52 (0.15)	0.01	20	0.53
4.3 Business Assoc.	3.00 (0.01)	3.21*** (0.00)	0.78 (0.44)	0.00	20	0.49
One-tailed tests, assuming equal variances. (p-values in parentheses)		Significance levels: * = 10 percent level; ** = 5 percent level; *** = 1 percent level.				

Figure 4.2:   Media Repression
Media repression is based on the Press Freedom Survey as presented in Sussman (1999). It is an index of many dimensions of media repression. All countries in Figure 1.4 are included in Figure 4.2. See Table A.6 for an indication of simple statistical significance.

Figure 4.3:   Business Associations and Corruption
All data are based on the BEEPS. All countries in Figure 1.4 are included in Figure 4.3. See Table A.6 for an indication of simple statistical significance.

Chapter 5. Designing Effective Anticorruption Strategies

Figure 5.3:   The chart is from Anderson (2000). It is based on a survey of 400 enterprise managers in the Slovak Republic carried out in 1999 by the Focus Agency for the World Bank and USAID.

Figure 5.4:   These charts are based on diagnostic surveys undertaken in Albania (see Kaufmann, Prasha, Preci, Ryterman, and Zoido-Lobaton (1998)), Georgia (see Anderson, Azfar, Kaufmann, Lee, and Mukherjee (1998)), Latvia (see Anderson (1998)), and the Slovak Republic (see Anderson (2000)). Several of the surveys were supported by USAID. The Albania public officials survey was undertaken by ACER in 1998, and had a sample size of 97. The Georgia enterprise survey was undertaken by GORBI in 1998 and had a sample size of 350. The Latvia household survey was undertaken by Latvia Facts in 1998 and had a sample size of 1,100. The Slovak Republic public officials survey was undertaken by Focus is 1999 and had a sample size of 350.

Chapter 6. Conclusion

Figure 6.1:   Change in the Extent of Bribery During the Last 5 Years
The data used to create Figure 6.1 are from the Global Competitiveness Survey, World Economic Forum, available at http://www.weforum.org. The chart was kindly provided by Daniel Kaufmann.

www.ingramcontent.com/pod-product-compliance
Lightning Source LLC
Chambersburg PA
CBHW080335270326
41927CB00014B/3228